William Brough

Open Mints and Free Banking

William Brough

Open Mints and Free Banking

ISBN/EAN: 9783337114343

Printed in Europe, USA, Canada, Australia, Japan

Cover: Foto ©Suzi / pixelio.de

More available books at **www.hansebooks.com**

WITH THE
COMPLIMENTS OF THE AUTHOR

OPEN MINTS AND FREE BANKING

BY

WILLIAM BROUGH

Author of "The Natural Law of Money"

"*Individuality* is left out of their scheme of government. The *State* is all in all."—BURKE.

G. P. PUTNAM'S SONS
NEW YORK & LONDON
The Knickerbocker Press
1898

The Knickerbocker Press, New York

PREFACE.

THIS little book, begun in the summer of 1896, was originally planned in the form of two magazine articles, but I soon found that to fully set forth my reasons for the changes I suggest in our monetary laws would involve a more extended discussion of principles than could be compressed into the space at command. This change of plan, occurring when the excitement of a pending Presidential election made dispassionate and unbiased writing as difficult as it was important, led to the laying aside of the work for a time; which fact explains why the statistics given in the book are not altogether up to date. But as the figures are used only to illustrate my argument, and as the deductions drawn from them would not be altered by later statements, I have allowed them to stand.

The essential point of difference between the theory of money here presented and the theories upon which monetary legislation has generally been framed, is the abolishment of a legally fixed ratio of value for gold and silver coin. I am fully convinced that if this theory were put into practice, its adoption would place gold and silver money upon an absolutely equal footing; it would take the Government altogether out of banking business, and would give to the currency the largest possible degree of elasticity; and this without disturbance to business and without inflicting injustice upon individuals such as, under our present monetary laws, would inevitably follow a suspension of gold payment.

In discussing the principles involved, I have found it necessary to give a more definite meaning to the word *money*, and to the term *the circulation*, than is to be found in the dictionaries. The word money, when not otherwise qualified, is used in the sense of being the measure of value in common use. As the copper, nickel, and minor silver coinage is used only for making change, and is not the measure of value, no special reference has been made to it.

W. B.

NEW YORK, January, 1898.

CONTENTS.

CHAPTER I.

INTRODUCTORY 1-33

An attempt to outline briefly a plan of monetary reorganization for the United States on a scientific basis—What the advocates of the different standards may justly claim—Edward Atkinson's statement as to the annual product of silver—Bimetallism—Lord Liverpool's *Coins of the Realm*—John Locke on *Lowering of Interest*—How the two metals may be retained in service—Token money—The creation of a single standard of value—The Bank of France—Co-operation of nations to establish a fixed ratio—How the parity of silver and gold money is maintained—What constitutes money—What is meant by the circulation—The duty of the Government in regard to money—The Greenback party—Importance of a self-regulating currency shown by the panics of 1893—Proposed reform in our monetary laws.

CHAPTER II.

THE GRESHAM LAW 34-41

"Good" and "bad" money—Stability in value the most important quality of money—Effect of a legal ratio—Extended use of silver as money—Jevons on the Gresham Law—Free coinage as a regulator—Evil effects of governmental interference.

CHAPTER III.

MONEY, CAPITAL, AND BANKING . . . 42–67

Characteristics and office of paper money—National and State bank notes—How to modify the inelasticity of government paper money—Scotch system of free banking—Canadian system of banking—The proper functions of a bank—On bank-note issue—Floating and fixed capital—Comparison of the note issue and the deposits of the Bank of Dundee—Local paper money—Bank auditing—Comparison of separate and independent banks with the parent system—Objections to the parent system.

CHAPTER IV.

ARGUMENTS IN SUPPORT OF THE PROPOSED LEGISLATIVE CHANGES 68–79

As to the discrimination between the different issues of government paper money—How to ensure stability—Popular preference for government notes—Normal relative proportion of paper to metallic money—Why it is difficult to maintain the gold reserve—The Bland Act—A review of our monetary legislation.

CHAPTER V.

THE PRECIOUS METALS AS AFFECTED IN THEIR RELATIVE VALUE BY PRODUCTION AND BY DEMONETIZATION 80–91

Cause of the variation in the relative value of the precious metals—Elements which give stability to the precious metals—Dr. Soetbeer's tables of production of the precious metals—Additional tables published by the Fourth National Bank of New York—Deductions from foregoing tables—Relative stability of gold and silver.

CHAPTER VI.

ON THE STANDARD OF VALUE 92–107

First formal discussion of monetary standards in 1867—The signification of standard of value and of unit of account—Advantage of a universal monetary unit—Decision of the Paris Convention—Germany the first to demonetize silver—Classification of nations according to their monetary systems—The demonetization of silver—Action of the Bank of France in preserving relative value—The hoarding spirit in France—Formation and object of the Latin Union—Gold monometallism in England—Deterioration of silver coin in England—Suspension of silver coinage in England.

CHAPTER VII.

HYBRID METALLISM 108–126

Evolvement of a new system of metallic money—Its working in Holland—The gold standard adopted by Holland in 1873—England the only nation that fully maintains the gold standard—Requirements of hybrid metallism—Powers derived by the precious metals from their use as money—Demonetization of silver in India—What would result from making gold the universal standard—Effect upon silver of demonetization—Effect upon gold of the demonetization of silver—Temptation to adopt hybrid metallism—Objections to hybrid metallism.

CHAPTER VIII.

CREDIT AS A MONETARY FACTOR, ILLUSTRATED IN THE WORKING OF THE ENGLISH MONETARY SYSTEM 127–172

The function of credit—Over-production an effect, not a cause—Effect of a sudden contraction of credit, and of a sudden withdrawal of floating capital—Difference between a capital and a currency panic—The floating capital of the country largely owned by the working class, but administered by the bankers—A superabundance of capital impossible—What governs the rate of interest—The English banking system considered—Monopolistic banking contrasted with independent banking—Weakness of the one-reserve system—Conditions in the United States favorable to the introduction of a free system of money—Clearing-house associations—Condition of economic knowledge in England when the Bullion Report was made—Analysis of the Bullion Report—Service rendered by the Bullion Committee—Sir Robert Peel's bribe to the Scottish bankers—The two departments of the Bank of England—Total issue of Bank of England notes—Peel's theory of trade—Speculation the only over-trading—Cause of the panic of 1847—Effect of restriction of interchange and of credit—Production the final object of trade activities—Concluding considerations of the banking law of England—The panic of 1847 a capital panic—Bank of England's rate of discount—England's supremacy in the financial world due to the sense of security she inspires—How the silver question may be settled.

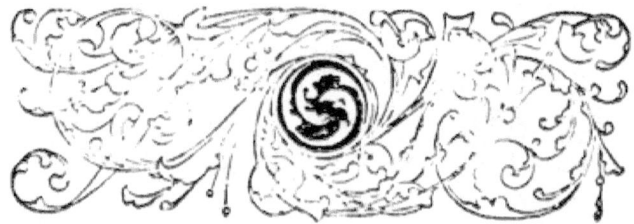

OPEN MINTS AND FREE BANKING

OPEN MINTS AND FREE BANKING.

CHAPTER I.

INTRODUCTORY.

THE following is an attempt to outline briefly and in essentials only, a plan of monetary reorganization for the United States, which shall not only be sound but practicable, in that it takes into consideration the present condition of the currency, and the varying or conflicting views of the different political parties in regard to money, and also that it aims to furnish a scientific basis for the solution of the problem.

This work is undertaken in the belief that these differences are rather seeming than real, and that a careful consideration of the nature and function of money, of credit, and of the distinction between money and capital, would show that the view of each party is founded upon at least one essential monetary principle, and that a relinquishment of non-essentials by each party would open the way to a satisfactory adjustment of the whole question. It is assumed that no plan would now be practicable that does not embody first, the essential principles of the advocates of the gold standard, second, of the advocates of free-silver coinage, and third, of that large body of American citizens who regard government paper money as superior to bank-notes.

The advocates of the gold standard may rightfully insist that our present circulation, which has been upon a gold basis since January 1, 1879, shall, when retired, be redeemed in gold; but it is not necessary to the accomplishment of this end that the English monetary system, which practically excludes silver money, should be imposed upon this country. That system is itself by no means perfect, and neither adapted nor adaptable to the conditions existing in the United States.

The advocates of silver may justly insist upon free coinage as a monetary principle that should never be violated; but as this principle has in fact already been violated—with honest intention, let us admit—and as opening the mints to free coinage, so long as the law declaring a parity of sixteen to one is still in existence, would bring disaster and discredit upon the nation, the silver advocates should certainly agree that provision must first be made for the maintenance of the present circulation until its retirement, at its nominal value in gold.

To the advocates of government paper money, it may be said in passing, that under the plan of reform hereinafter set forth, no paper money can come into general circulation that is not as sound as government paper money; nor can any paper money displace the government money unless, in addition to its soundness, it possesses a larger measure of elasticity. Our paper circulation is now substantially all government money, which flows in and out of the Treasury, not in sympathy with the state of trade, but dependent solely upon the receipts and expenditures of the government; hence this inflow and outflow are of a purely mechanical character, and the currency has no elasticity—no adaptability to the requirements of trade. This lack of elasticity in government money is at once a serious embarrassment to the Treasury Department, and a constant menace to industrial prosperity.

National bank notes are practically a government issue, the Government having assumed the entire control of, and responsibility for them. The National banks are under no obligation to redeem their notes in the metallic standard, nor must these specific notes be retired for the purpose of lifting the bonds pledged with the Government for their redemption; for this may be, and usually is, done with other than their own notes. Then the notes, which are supposed to be retired, wander about like so many tramps until it suits the convenience of the Government to retire them. There are now in the circulation about twenty million dollars of these so-called "retired" notes, which have no more responsiveness for their special work of imparting elasticity to the currency than tramps have for any work.

In order to appreciate the nature of our subject, we must dismiss from our minds the idea, so commonly presented in popular discussion, that the demand for silver money is of a purely personal character, and that it is prompted solely by selfish motives. For instance, it is usually assumed that the silver-mine owners originated the movement and are impelling it for their private gain; also that the debtor farmers see in a change to silver an easy way of discharging their mortgage indebtedness; but these assumptions will not bear dispassionate investigation.

Edward Atkinson informs us that the annual product of silver in the United States is not quite half of one per cent. of the total annual wealth product, and the same trustworthy authority, having investigated the mortgage indebtedness of farmers, finds it to be a mere fraction of the total interest that this large class has in maintaining the monetary integrity of the country. Moreover, it should be kept in mind that the demand for silver money is not confined to the United States, but exists in England, France, Germany, and other countries which have adopted gold alone as their monetary standard. The silver agitation is too persistent, too widespread, and has been too long continued to derive its momentum or to find its sufficient reason either in individual dishonesty or in narrow selfishness.

A more rational hypothesis is that both bimetallism and monometallism, which have only come into existence as distinctive systems within the last eighty years, have in them radical defects which the inexorable logic of events is proceeding to eradicate. Bimetallism had previously a formative existence, but could not properly be called a system as now understood; for though European governments, in issuing silver and gold coins from the mints, always ordered the taking of these coins at a fixed ratio of value, the coinage laws were rarely enforced so as to compel the taking of the pieces at such ratio. In our own country no systematic effort was ever made by the Government to maintain silver and gold coins in circulation at a fixed ratio until the passage of the Bland Act in 1878. The Act of 1792 did indeed declare the ratio to be fifteen of silver to one of gold, and the Act of 1834 in like manner declared the ratio to be sixteen to one; but in neither instance were these ratios enforced in practice. The only effect of the former Act was to drive gold from the circulation because it was undervalued by the ratio fixed, and the only effect of the latter Act was to drive out silver for a similar reason.

Do not these examples furnish conclusive evidence that the radical defect in the system of bimetallism is the adoption of a ratio at which the two metals shall be an equivalent tender ? With a fixed ratio, one of the metals is sure to retire from the circulation if its market value is not in exact accord with the ratio, for no one will pay out the more valuable coin if one of less value can be made to serve his purpose. It was a recognition of this fact, coupled with the idea that if the two metals were not held at a legal ratio but were permitted to circulate independently, there would be two diverse and discordant measures of value, which led England to adopt gold for her monetary standard, with silver as merely subsidiary coinage.

Though not altogether oblivious of the fact that the market value of the precious metals regulated the value of the coins, there was nevertheless a vague sentiment pervading the universal mind, through the whole period of monarchy, even down to the present time, that the stamp of the Sovereign upon the pieces did in some measure contribute to fix their value. The essential fact is that the true and only function of the stamp is to certify the weight and purity of the precious metal in the coins. The perception of this principle has been obscured by the delusive theory that sovereignty can impart value to the pieces. That the coined metals cannot serve as a measure of value, unless the coins are permitted to pass at the market value of the metal they contain, is even now clearly perceived only by the few.

It was not until after the publication, in 1805, of Lord Liverpool's book entitled *The Coins of the Realm*, that the views entertained in relation to money had taken a form sufficiently definite to be called a system. A careful reading of this book shows that notwithstanding the author's recognition of the preponderating influence of the bullion market, he was still thoroughly possessed by the common belief that the current value of the coin was fixed by the monarch, whose unquestioned prerogative it was. Experience had taught him, however, that a legalized ratio between the two metals was frequently disturbed by the influence of the bullion market; he therefore came to the conclusion that only *one* metal should be retained as the common measure of value, and that the other should be deprived of that function. He selected gold as the metal that should be retained, and his theory was practically adopted and became the monetary law of England in 1816.

John Locke, whose essays on the *Lowering of Interest and Raising the Value of Money* were published in London in 1691, had a much clearer perception of the true nature of money than had Lord Liverpool. Locke clearly realized that it was the quantity of precious metal alone which gave coin its specific value and its purchasing power. In his day, silver was the money of every commercial nation. Recognizing this fact, and the fact that silver alone constituted the common measure of value for these nations, he advised that no value should be put upon gold coins when issued from the mints, but that they should be permitted to take their current value from the bullion market.

Lord Liverpool states that it was by the advice of Locke that the English government refrained from enforcing the circulation of the guinea at the mint indenture, which was twenty shillings. This piece was first issued in the reign of Charles the Second, and remained in circulation until the reign of George the Third; but during this long interval it never passed for less than twenty-one shillings. During the reign of William the Third (1689–1702) it passed for a time at a rate as high as thirty shillings, not because the value of gold had risen, but because the silver money, by which the value of the guinea was measured, had been reduced in weight, and consequently in value, by abrasion and clipping. When in this reign the silver coinage was restored to full weight (1696), the guinea fell to twenty-one shillings and sixpence. John Locke clearly foresaw that to force the taking of these pieces at the mint indenture of twenty shillings would drive them from the circulation, as the gold coins would then certainly be melted or exported by those who held them, but who were not permitted to pay them out at their market value.

The fundamental principle of metallic money, so

clearly set forth by Locke two hundred years ago—that the stamp of the Sovereign cannot alter the value of the coin, that it simply verifies the quantity and quality of precious metal in the piece—goes to the very root of our present monetary misunderstandings. It is still a common belief that the stamp of the Government is sufficient in itself to maintain the parity of the two metals, and we frequently read in leading newspapers of the Eastern States such misleading statements as that free coinage would enable silver-mine owners to obtain for their bullion, by coining it, the present current value of the silver dollar instead of its market value. Such statements are calculated only to widen the breach between the East on the one side and the South and West on the other, and to make the question, already sufficiently complex, still more difficult of solution.

Absolutely free coinage would place the silver-miner in a similar position to that now occupied by the gold-miner with reference to marketing his product; he would have to accept the market price for his silver whether he coined it or not. When there is a demand for gold coin, the gold-miner finds that he gains a small percentage in price by coining his bullion; but that the mint is not always his best

Introductory

market is evidenced by the fact that much of the gold produced in the United States is exported in bars. Nor are the silver-mine owners under any delusion on this point. Senator Jones of Nevada is doubtless a fair exponent of their views, and we may learn what these views are from his published speech, delivered before the United States Senate, May 12 and 13, 1890. As a silver-producer he neither asks nor expects to receive a bounty on his product.[1] He claims that the demonetization of silver by our Government, and by the governments of the leading commercial nations of Europe, has had the effect to advance the price of gold in the markets of the world, but not to lower the price of silver, and that consequently the purchasing power of gold money has been greatly enhanced, while that of silver money has remained stationary.

We need not follow Senator Jones through his elaborate and evidently conscientious argument in support of his theory, as it would lead us away from our subject; it should be added, however, that his advocacy of free coinage is for both metals, and not for silver alone.

---

[1] " . . . coins, the value of which coincided with the bullion value, which must necessarily be the case when free coinage is permitted."—Printed speech, p. 9.

Other writers contend that the fall in price of leading commodities (mainly farm products), which Senator Jones quotes as taking place between the years 1873 and 1889, was the result of cheaper methods of production and of cheaper transportation, and not that gold had risen in price in those years. The truth lies between these two claims. That the demonetization of silver would necessarily tend to advance the price of gold is unquestionably true, and on the other hand that there has been a cheapening in methods of production and in transportation is also true.

The problem before the American people, so urgently pressing for an answer, is *how to bring silver into monetary service on the same footing as gold, and how to retain both metals in circulation so that they shall be equally sound money.* In dealing with this problem we are confronted at the outset by two distinct phases of the question, one economic, the other ethic. To bring these metals into use so that they shall be equally sound money, involves the economical side of the question; to do this without wronging any one, involves the ethical side. That the people will insist upon the retention of both metals can hardly be questioned, but that they would adopt dishonest methods to attain an end which may be honestly achieved, is beyond belief. Individual instances of narrow selfishness and dishonesty are never lacking, but the nation, as a body, is honest, and must be so to preserve its existence.

Now there is but one way whereby the two metals may be retained in service as money, and that is by the repeal of all Acts which make them an equivalent tender at a given ratio; the coins of both metals would thereupon pass at their market value and would be a legal tender only at that value. It may be asked, "Could our monetary unit—the dollar—be represented in the circulation by two coins of unequal value without creating confusion?" The answer is that when coins of the two metals are left free to circulate at their market value, both cannot circulate as money in the same community, though each will circulate in that community to which it is adapted. The United States is a political but not necessarily an industrial entity. Industrially it is an agglomeration of diverse communities, and this being a natural condition, each community would select for use as money the metal best adapted to its needs.

Money is not merely a medium of exchange, it is primarily a measure of value, and it is only when one of the precious metals performs this service for a whole community that it becomes money in the true sense. A community may adopt either metal as its money, and the metal not chosen may circulate and perform important service, but it cannot be the measure of value for that community, because it will itself be measured by the metal selected as the common standard. No instance can be found in monetary history where the two metals have both served as a measure of value for the same community at the same time, but many instances can be cited where both have circulated in the same community, the one as money and the other in a subordinate capacity. Too much legislative meddling with the precious metals has prevented a general and clear preception of this natural law.

When a metal has become the money of a community, the coin of that metal will pass current at its market value, and must do so in order to perform its functions fully and efficiently; whenever the metal not so selected is made to pass at a higher than its bullion value, it is thereby deprived of its quality as a measure of value, and becomes only a local medium of exchange. This coin is sometimes called token money; a more appropriate name would be " crippled capital." Not having intrinsic value equal to its nominal value, it does not stimulate the wage-earner to exertion, as true metallic money does; he cannot send it out of the country without incurring loss, neither can he hoard it if he so desires; it is destructive of that sense of property-possession which is so wholesome in its effect upon the workingman as an incentive to industry—an effect that all true metallic money produces.

A single standard of value cannot be created by a legislative decree directing that the two metals shall be current only at a given ratio; for, upon the slightest market divergence from the ratio adopted, the undervalued metal will inevitably begin to pass out of circulation. The experience of France, which is presented by bimetallists as a complete illustration of the theory that two metals can be thus linked together, not only is not an exception to, but furnishes a signal exemplification of the fact that they cannot be so united. The bimetallic system prevailed in France at a ratio of fifteen and a half of silver to one of gold from 1803 to 1873; though the statute remains, it became practically inoperative through the closing of the mints against silver in the latter year. During this period of seventy years, the relative market value of the two metals ranged between 15.21 to one and 15.90 to one; these variations may seem small, but they were sufficient to prevent the two metals from constituting one standard measure of value. While the tables of prices show that the relative market value of the two metals was remarkably close throughout the whole period of seventy years, these tables also show that that value was rarely, if ever, in exact accord with the legal ratio. As the law permitted payment in the coin of either metal, the Bank of France always paid out the cheaper, parting with the other only at a premium; these variations were consequently made a source of great profit to the bank. Whenever a people have to pay more for one of the metals than the ratio fixed by law, the fact proves in itself that that metal has ceased to be their measure of value.

It cannot be questioned that the action of the Bank of France in always paying out the cheaper metal and selling the other at a profit contributed to preserve uniformity in the relative value of the two metals; but let us ask in what respect did the method adopted by the Bank of France differ from that of any individual who deals in these metals? The bank was governed solely by the incentive of profit, and would it not be so governed if there were no legal ratio at which coins of the two metals must be accepted? Profit is the motive which governs every man in his financial dealings; consequently profit is the natural regulator whereby the metals are held at a steady relative value.

As there is a very general belief that, if the leading commercial nations can be induced to co-operate, the two metals may be held at a fixed relative value, it would be interesting to have some one explain the particular process whereby this feat is to be accomplished. We dismiss, of course, the idea that value can be created by a *fiat* decree of one nation or of any number of nations combined; and if value cannot be thus created, a fixed ratio, which is merely the relation between values, certainly cannot be established. A current fixed relative value may be given to gold and silver coins by redeeming the coin of lower market value in the coin of higher market value; but this process would surely prove burdensome to the nations undertaking it. An international clearing-house would therefore be needed to hold each nation to its pro rata share of the burden. The proposition is too impracticable to be entertained; it is furthermore utterly incompatible with the natural course of trade and finance.

When the precious metals are freed from legislative interference, one of them naturally and inevitably becomes the standard of value of the community to the exclusion of the other metal as such standard. Why then should we struggle to keep them linked together? No one would yoke together a race-horse and a draught-horse in the expectation of thus utilizing and combining the merits of the two; he would recognize that the usefulness of both horses would be impaired by such union, and that only by using them separately could the speed of the one and the strength of the other be made effective as well as co-operative in the true sense. This illustration indicates the relation of the money metals; for while together they constitute the money of the civilized world, and while it is unquestionably true that their similarity and interchangeability contribute largely to keep their relative value steady, yet it is equally true that their differing qualifications as money metals are sufficient to lead each community to adopt as its measure of value that one which best serves its particular needs.

If a combination of the leading commercial nations were practicable, the only way in which such combination could contribute to hold the precious metals at a steady ratio of value would be, when that ratio was disturbed, to pay out the cheaper metal and part with the other only at a premium, precisely as was done by the Bank of France prior to 1873. But this is what every individual who handles these metals does when he can, entirely irrespective of any laws that may be enacted and of any combinations that may be formed. Is it not evident then that what is needed is not combinations, but relief from existing restrictive and obstructive monetary laws? The only effective agent is individual action prompted by the incentive of profit, and such action would be universal if the metals were free.

It will be seen from what has already been said, that the only condition upon which gold and silver can be retained in circulation is that the coin of each metal shall pass at its bullion value. In order to effect this, it will be necessary to repeal all Acts which declare these metals to be an equivalent tender; to open the mints for the free coinage of silver as well as of gold, and to continue the redemption of silver money in gold until the present silver circulation shall be retired; and to that extent and for that purpose only.

Since January 1, 1879, our Government has stood ready at all times to redeem greenbacks and Treasury notes in gold, and this has practically resulted in maintaining silver, whether in coined dollars or represented by paper, at a parity with gold dollars, because no one has had any difficulty in obtaining for his silver money the notes that are specifically redeemable in gold.

All the purchasing power above their bullion value possessed by the silver dollars in circulation is derived from three conditions—first, that they are practically redeemable in gold money; second, creditors must accept them when tendered in payment; third, they may be used in payment of taxes. It is, however, by the first condition alone that the parity is maintained; for should the Government fail to redeem them in gold money, the moment the fact became known they would begin to depreciate in their current value. Their availability in payment of debts and taxes would indeed for a time maintain for them a current value somewhat above their worth as bullion, but notwithstanding this, they would ultimately and inevitably pass at their bullion value, whatever that might be.

Now if the mints were opened for free coinage of silver without provision having first been made for the redemption in gold money of all our present silver currency, there would be a run upon the Treasury for gold which would compel the Government to discontinue payments in that metal; in which event the legislative Acts referred to could have no effect but to prevent the return of gold to the Treasury and general circulation. This condition would continue so long as these Acts remained in force, and so long as the market value of the gold dollar was greater than the current value of the silver dollar. Hence it follows that in order to retain coin of both metals in circulation, the Acts which decree these metals to be an equivalent tender must be repealed; and in order to avoid bringing discredit upon the nation by any injustice, our Government must, before opening the mints to the free coinage of silver, provide for the retirement of the present silver currency in the metal which it represents, and which has been our only measure of value since 1879, namely, gold.

Strictly speaking, our current silver is not money, for money is the measure of value which is in general use, in the same sense that the yard-stick is a measure of length, the bushel a measure of bulk, and the pound a measure of weight. The name *money* properly refers to the service performed rather than to the agency which performs it; whatever that agency may be, it is money only when employed by a nation or community as the common measure of value. That which we call silver money, as it is redeemable in gold, is in effect gold money; hence gold alone has been our money since 1879. The entire volume of currency, including all the different forms of paper money and the coined silver dollars, being readily convertible into gold either directly or by a second turn, is therefore substantially gold money.

So much vagueness exists in the public mind in reference to the term "the circulation," that it may be well to explain what is here meant by that term. The words are used to express the whole volume of money in the service of a nation at any given time. The precious metals in a country are not always in such service, and when they are not in such service they are capital and not money. Coining these metals does not necessarily make them money. As will be shown later, the silver in the vaults of the United States Treasury, coined or uncoined, performs no monetary service whatever; it is therefore not in the circulation, it is capital held in idleness. On the other hand, the gold in the Treasury, whether in bars or in coin, is in service as money, and is consequently in the circulation. When an army is engaged in battle, the reserve force of that army is as necessary a part of the whole as are the men who are actually fighting, and in such case it may be truly said that "he also serves who only stands and waits." Similarly, the gold which may never leave the vaults of the Treasury is at all times in the active service of the nation as money, so long as gold is our monetary standard, and so long as it is held there to maintain the paper or representative money that is out.

Again, the gold belonging to National banks is capital and not money, because this gold does nothing to maintain the integrity of the currency, since the National banks are not under the legal obligation that they should be to redeem their notes in gold. This gold, however, is not idle capital as is the silver in the vaults of the Treasury, because it serves to strengthen the credit of the banks, and to extend their usefulness in sustaining the activities of their customers. All money of whatever form or character, whether in the pockets of the people, the till of the shopkeeper, the safe of the banker, or wherever it may be, if held for expenditure and not hoarded, is in " the circulation."

It may be set down as a universal and fundamental economic law that under normal conditions the volume of money in circulation will always be equal to the commercial needs, and as the sum of these needs is constantly changing, this volume will expand and contract in unison with the varying demand. As no government can foresee what these varying needs will be, no government can provide for them, hence the supplying of money should be left to the local industrial and trading communities as these needs arise. That government's course is most wholesome that interferes least with this natural law, confining itself to such services as will facilitate and not impede the operation of the law. A government may properly be the agent for coining the precious metals, because its stamp on the coin furnishes a satisfactory guaranty of weight and fineness, and to protect the public against counterfeit coin is a government's plain duty; but it cannot exceed these functions, nor can it supply paper money, without coming into direct conflict with the growth of industry.

Every one who has given this subject any study knows that money should possess the quality of elasticity, but how to secure for a nation a currency so elastic that it will respond to every legitimate demand upon it in every locality where industry is possible, is still but imperfectly understood. As the only function of money is to effect exchanges, the volume of currency cannot at any given time be increased beyond the amount needed for that purpose without lowering its value and impairing its efficiency; nor can it be diminished without arresting some industry. We may throw the mints wide open to the freest coinage of silver and gold, and no more of these metals will be coined than is actually needed for the monetary service of the country. Why? Simply because the coined metal would then pass current at its intrinsic value, and bullion would be taken to the mints only when the owners could get for it a better price if coined than by selling it in open market. A very small percentage of difference over the price that can be obtained in open market is sufficient to attract bullion to a free mint, and to encourage the coining of it until the coin in circulation is brought in value to the level of the bullion market. On the other hand, if more bullion is coined than is actually needed for monetary service, the coinage sinks in value below the bullion market, and the surplus coin is melted down either for export or for use in the arts at home. In this natural way the coinage is kept at a value level with the bullion market, and it thus acquires greater stability than can be given to it by any artificial regulative process. The bullion market is the true regulator; it has magnitude, expansiveness, and freedom, elements requisite to produce steadiness in the price of any commodity.

Only evil can result from a State's undertaking to furnish the circulating medium; for it is not within the power of the State to adjust the supply to the needs, and unless this is accomplished, the industrial organism cannot be in healthful working order. If the money issued by the State is at any given time in excess of the needs, and if there is no natural outlet for the excess, it will find its way to the centres of trade, to be used in speculative gambling operations. If the excess is greater than can be absorbed in this way, it will force a free outlet by sinking the entire circulation below its nominal value, until the volume at such value is no greater than the needs. The operation of this law was fully illustrated during the war period, when inconvertible paper was our only money.

On the other hand, if the volume of money issued by the State is at any given time insufficient, and the people are debarred from other sources of supply, the circulation will rise in value until the volume becomes sufficient for the needs. As all values are relative, it is only by comparing the worth of one commodity with that of another that we acquire an idea of value. Hence a rise in the value of the currency would be equivalent to a general decline in prices. In bartering one commodity for another, we plainly perceive their relative value; but having adopted one commodity as the measure (the money) for all other commodities, we become accustomed to regard that measure as constant and unvarying in value, and to the common mind it seems to be only the other commodities that rise and fall in price. This being the case, it is obviously of the first importance that money should have a steady value, for if it lack this quality, such persons as do not perceive its fluctuations (and they are the great mass of producers) are constantly exposed in their trading to loss of property and to consequent discouragement; the ultimate effect of these fluctuations being to aggregate into few hands an undue proportion of the wealth produced. No State can be healthy unless the conditions of distribution are as satisfactory as those of production; a government cannot restrict the freedom of the people in the choice of the money they shall use, nor can it limit the volume below the needs of trade, without entailing the evils referred to.

To a modern industrial community, money is as the breath of life, and the State can no more regulate the supply of the people's money than it can regulate the volume of air the people breathe. This phase of the question is not yet fully appreciated even by many eminent economists and bankers. The conditions out of which the Greenback Party arose furnish a significant illustration of the evil effects of an attempt by our Government arbitrarily to contract the volume of currency. The aim of the Government was to bring about a resumption of specie payments by the retirement of all government paper money, and to preclude the possibility of the issue of notes by any other than the National banks. The retirement of the greenbacks was undertaken at a time when the National banks were very unequally distributed throughout the country, especially in the South and West, and when they were too few in number and too weak in capital to replace the retired currency. To effect the purpose of the Government, an Act was passed March 3, 1865, imposing a tax of ten per cent. on every issue of State-bank notes, and on all other paper money not expressly sanctioned by the Government at Washington. A supplementary Act, passed April 12, 1866, required the retirement of the greenback circulation at a rate not exceeding $10,000,000 for the first six months, nor above $4,000,000 per month thereafter. These Acts were practically prohibitory in their terms, for the people had no means of obtaining a sufficient supply of legal money except by paying a tax of ten per cent. on all notes issued other than government or National, bank notes, or the alternative of paying fifty per cent. premium for gold money, which was the average premium ruling at the time, as measured by current money.

We can now see that no other possible effect could have followed such legislation than that which did follow. The people were quietly pursuing their accustomed avocations, giving but little attention to any monetary measures that Congress might adopt, until the scarcity occasioned by the withdrawal of the greenbacks became oppressive, when there arose a great outcry, and a demand for the repeal of the Act directing the contraction of the currency. The people of the Eastern States have called this outcry and demand for money " the greenback craze." In a sense different from that intended, it was indeed a craze, for there is nothing more likely to drive a people to madness than to wreck them in their business enterprises, and such wrecking cannot be more effectively accomplished than by contracting the currency below the needs.

Another illustration of the importance of a self-regulative currency was given by the panics of 1893, for it must be specially noted that in that year there were two panics arising from distinctly different causes, that of May being emphatically a capital panic, and that of August as emphatically a currency panic. The former was brought on by the withdrawal from industrial employment of a large amount of capital belonging to foreign and home investors, a withdrawal consequent upon a general fear among the people that the Government might be unable to maintain the gold standard. The May panic put a stop to all contemplated enterprises, to a considerable extent arrested active industries, and compelled economy in consumption; but wherever capital was not lacking, business went on, and the industrial organism remained intact. The August panic was caused by the hoarding of currency, and its workings were altogether different. The withdrawal of needed money from the circulation operates destructively upon industry, and with a force out of all proportion to the amount withdrawn. In this crisis the amount withdrawn by the hoarding was sufficient to have thrown the whole industry of the nation into collapse, had not the catastrophe been averted by the prompt action of the people, who in total disregard of the ten per cent. tax, created a currency for themselves. Due-bills in the form of bank-notes were issued by manufacturing companies, by clearing-house associations, by railroads, by banks, and by individuals.[1]

Nor was this all that was done to replace the circulation and to avert a complete collapse of the nation's industries. From forty to fifty million dollars in gold were imported at great expense, and it is said that in order to secure legal money, one New York bank incurred a loss of $50,000. This incident affords evidence of the terrible struggle of the banks to maintain their existence through the crisis. In the city of New York individual bank-checks became for a time the circulating medium and measure of value for the city. Throughout the month of August all prices were quoted in this standard, and legal money was measured by it, commanding a premium which rose as high as four per cent. This panic reached its greatest tension in the third week of August, and before the first of November, the day on which the silver-purchasing clauses of the Sherman Act were repealed, the industries which had been compelled to shut down for want of currency had resumed work; proving that such repeal, while it doubtless contributed to restore confidence

---

[1] Those who may wish to know more of the variety and extent of these issues should read a most interesting pamphlet by Jno. DeWitt Warner, entitled *The Currency Famine of 1893*, published by the Reform Club of New York

for a time, and thus to stay the outflow of capital, did nothing to relieve the August panic.

The inability of the National banks to cope with such a crisis was made manifest. They struggled as best they could in the limited sphere of action which their charters grant them, yet they accomplished little by the issue of new notes to relieve the pressure for currency, because before they could get bonds lodged with the Government and obtain therefor the quantum of notes allowed, the turning-point of the crisis had passed.

Before entering upon a detailed discussion of the principles involved, it seems desirable to present to the reader a statement of the changes necessary to be made in our monetary laws in order to bring about the proposed reform:

(1) Repeal all laws which make paper money a legal tender.

(2) Require the National banks to redeem on demand their notes in the metallic money which they represent, *i. e.*, gold.

(3) Repeal the Acts which make silver and gold dollars an equivalent tender.

(4) Repeal the Act of March 3, 1865, which prevents other than National banks from issuing notes, and require that all notes shall be redeemed on

demand at the counter of the bank issuing them, and in the metallic money which they represent.

(5) Open the mints to free coinage of both metals.

(6) Repeal the law which empowers the Secretary of the Treasury to redeem either in silver or in gold at his discretion, and transfer that choice to the holder of any United States money which may be brought to the Treasury for exchange or redemption.

(7) Repeal all laws which require or direct the Secretary of the Treasury to pay out and keep in circulation any specified kind of money.

(8) Definitely pledge the nation to the payment in gold money of all its present outstanding obligations.

CHAPTER II.

THE GRESHAM LAW.

A THEORY has been promulgated by economic writers that bad money will, under all circumstances, drive good money from the circulation, and this theory has been named the "Gresham Law." The words "good" and "bad," applied as they are by these writers to money in general, convey no specific meaning. Money varies in kind; one kind may be good money for one community, and yet not for another whose occupations are different. Money in general has no other use but to facilitate exchanges and thereby increase productiveness; the money which is most effective in accomplishing these ends must therefore be the best. But as differing communities require different kinds of money, it would be a misnomer to call a money bad, simply because, while rendering efficient service to one community, it would be inefficient if employed by another.

As money is the measure of value, the most important quality it can possess is stability in value, and this quality it derives from its metallic base. Silver and gold are the only metals that serve universally as money, and the action of these metals upon each other, through interchange, gives them greater stability than either could have singly. Demonetize one of them and the stability of the other is thereby impaired. It may be said that it would be bad to thus expel one metal from service, but the term " good " or " bad " would have no meaning if applied to the money of the metal remaining in service.

The truth is, that the economists who invented the Gresham Law had but a vague conception of the nature of money. In their minds the State alone was competent to supply and regulate the quantity and kinds needed. They regarded money from an outside standpoint, omitting to take into account the nature of the forces that act upon money from within. The more efficient money will always drive from the circulation the less efficient if the individuals who handle money are left free to act in their own interest. It is only when bad money is endowed by the State with the property of legal tender that it can drive good money from the circulation.

These economists have assumed that in order to obtain a single standard in any given community, it is necessary either to adopt a legal ratio at which the two precious metals shall be current, or to expel one from service as money. Failing to perceive that there is a natural law which permits only one metal to be the measure of value (the money) for a community, the necessity for an artificial bond of union between the two metals has seemed to them imperative; and starting from these false premises, they have been forced to assume that the universal law of self-interest, which impels improvement in all other implements of trade and industry, is, in the case of money, reversed. The position of these economists is not unlike that of the French nation, which, at the time when Newton promulgated the law of gravitation, maintained the theory that each planet was held in its orbit by a presiding angel divinely appointed to that duty. Walter Bagehot says it was fifty years after Newton's theory was announced before the French people could make up their minds to accept it, and dispense with these imaginary guardians.

The Gresham Law

The so-called Gresham Law becomes operative only when coins of unequal value are made an equivalent legal tender, and such conditions could not exist between gold and silver dollars passing at their intrinsic value, as each would be a legal tender at that value only. Gold coin passes now at its bullion value, and the change proposed would simply put silver coin on the same independent footing. Whenever the two metals are artificially tied together by legislation, the individual is always urged, by the natural law of self-interest, to untie them and to re-establish their inherent independence. For instance, when an individual has two coins of unequal value with either of which he may pay his debt, what is more natural than that he should pay with the coin which is of lower value, and keep the other? And he will do this entirely irrespective of the monetary merits of either coin. It is illogical, therefore, to seek to deduce from this a general law that says " bad money drives out good money, but good money cannot drive out bad money."[1] What the individual wants is the difference between the two coins, which to him is profit; meanwhile the coin which he withholds from the circulation and melts or exports may not be as effi-

[1] Jevons, *Money and the Mechanism of Exchange*, p. 82.

cient money for his community as the one with which he pays his debt, and which is thus kept in the circulation.

The only natural difference between the coins of the two metals is, that to express the same value a silver coin must be larger and heavier than a gold coin; and this difference is a great advantage if each community is free to choose for its monetary standard the metal best adapted to its needs. Silver at its market value is just as sound money as gold is at its market value, and if opportunity were given, undoubtedly all of our Southern and many of our Western States would select silver money as being better fitted for their use.

At least two thirds of the entire population of the globe are now using silver money, and it may safely be predicted not only that these nations will continue to do so indefinitely, but that other nations which have not yet reached the silver basis will eventually adopt it. For example, China's only legal money is copper, but she is gradually absorbing silver, and will in time undoubtedly reach the silver standard. Notwithstanding the efforts of European governments to enforce the exclusive use of gold money, it is a significant fact that in no single instance where gold money has been substituted for silver money, not even in England, as will be shown later, have the people themselves demanded the change. The gold standard has been imposed upon them by their governments, acting upon the mistaken views of the economists.

As Jevons may be said fairly to represent the views of economists generally on the subject of the Gresham Law, we quote from him again: "In matters of currency, self-interest acts in the opposite direction to what it does in other affairs," and "there is nothing less fit to be left to the action of competition than money."[1] "People want coin not to keep in their pockets, but to pass off into their neighbors' pockets, and the worse the money which they can get their neighbors to accept, the greater the profits to themselves." Hence he argues that deterioration of the metallic currency "can only be prevented by the constant supervision of the State."[2] This writer also calls in question the position taken by Herbert Spencer, who maintains that "the existing monetary system (of England) would be benefited by the withdrawal of State control."[3]

It is the testimony of history, that with free export

---

[1] Jevons, *Money and the Mechanism of Exchange*, p. 64.
[2] Jevons, *Money and the Mechanism of Exchange*, p. 82.
[3] *Social Statics* (edition of 1892), p. 228.

and import of the precious metals, and with free coinage, the coins of both metals will circulate at their bullion value; that both may circulate in one community at the same time—one as the monetary standard and the other as a medium of exchange—this medium being itself measured by that selected as the standard. That this natural law has been obscured from view is due to the fact that from remote times down to the present time every imaginable interference with the freedom of the money metals has been continually attempted. When these interferences shall cease it will be found that money comes under the same general law as that which brings about improvements in all other tools and implements, namely, through the action of individuals prompted by the incentive of profit. Cease to make coin a legal tender at a value which it does not possess intrinsically, and the chance for profit-making by " shoving " our bad money on our neighbors will cease also. We may freely admit that individuals will seek to pass off their bad coin upon their neighbors, but will the neighbors keep it and accept their loss, or will they in their turn pass it off on others ? How long would any community endure such a currency ? No community in our day would permit its coinage to become a cause of petty cheating and of constant higgling in every market-place, nor did any community in the past long tolerate the evil without protest and effort to rectify it. It soon becomes apparent that the interest of each member of the community is best subserved by mutual protection against such a curse, and steps are taken to secure for the community as a body a definite and stable measure of value. Search history, and it will be found that the people are always the first to protest against a deterioration of the currency, while it is generally the Sovereign or the Government that causes the deterioration either by direct spoliation or by false monetary legislation.

CHAPTER III.

MONEY, CAPITAL, AND BANKING.

TO permit the National banks to redeem their notes in other than the metallic money represented by the notes, at once involves a violation of a monetary principle and an abrogation of a governmental function. We have seen how essential it is that the circulation should at all times be exactly equal to the needs. Now if the currency is composed exclusively of metallic money, its expanding and contracting power, as a whole, is limited by the flow of the precious metals from and to other countries, and the demand for metallic money within the boundaries of our own country can be met only by transporting it from points where it is in excess to points where it is needed. It is only through such cumbersome processes that metallic money acquires the slight degree of elasticity it possesses. While metallic money seems to have fulfilled the requirements of earlier times, it began more than two hundred years ago to manifest its inadequacy to meet the growing and more complex conditions of modern trade; paper money then came into use. It is from paper money that the currency of a country acquires its largest measure of elasticity, but this paper must be in the form of bank-notes redeemable on demand in the metallic money they represent at the counter of the bank issuing them. Unless the paper money is of this kind, it may be even less elastic than a metallic currency.

While our Government paper currency is maintained at a cost equal to that of a gold currency, it does not and cannot possess as much elasticity as an exclusively gold currency, for it is governed in its flow from and to the Treasury only by the needs of the Government, without reference to the needs of the people. Nor can it flow out of or into the country in response to the needs of trade as gold does. In the Treasury Department the pulsations of the currency which proceed from the demands of trade are distinctly seen and felt, yet however much the Secretary may desire to respond to these demands, he can do so only to a very limited extent, because he is always handicapped by the necessities of the Government, to say nothing of the restrictive legislation which directs him to keep certain notes in circulation, whether they are wanted or not. A more rigid and inelastic currency than our Government paper money could not be devised.

The commonly entertained idea in reference to paper money is that the more extended the area over which the notes circulate and the longer they stay out, the better they are; whereas they should possess characteristics the opposite of these. They should circulate only within a limited radius of their point of redemption, so that they may be promptly retired when not wanted, and brought out again as promptly when wanted; and they will so circulate if made payable on demand in the metallic standard at the counter of the bank issuing them. A mixed currency of paper and coin best fulfils all the conditions required, and under a properly organized system of free coinage and free banking we should have such a currency. There are about nine thousand banks, State and National, in the United States, each one of which is an industrial outgrowth of the particular locality and is necessary to its prosperity. If all these banks were free to issue notes on their own credit and without bonded security, there would always be a sufficiency of currency, and if it were obligatory on these banks to redeem their notes in metallic money on demand, the currency would never exceed the needs. Banking is so often regarded as an occult mystery rather than as an ordinary commercial business, that it may seem incredible to some that these simplifying changes in banking laws could produce such beneficial results; but the statement does not rest upon theory alone; history furnishes at least two marked illustrations of the theory verified in practice.

In 1716, after twenty-one years of monopolistic banking, Scotland adopted a system of free banking, which left the business, as all other branches of trade and industry were left, to be worked out by the people in their own way; and the result was the best system of banking that has ever existed. Not understanding the elementary principles of note issue—that credit must rest on confidence and can have no element of force in it—the banks at first made their notes payable six months from date of issue, but if a note was presented for redemption before maturity, it was either redeemed at sight or interest was paid on it for the remainder of its term. The error of issuing time-notes was rectified in 1765 by an Act of Parliament which made it obligatory upon the banks to redeem them on demand in the metallic standard. By the same Act the banks were prohibited from issuing notes of a denomination below one pound sterling. These were the only legislative changes made from absolute free banking until 1845, when the future issuance of notes against which there was no legal obligation to hold a metallic money reserve was limited to the amount which the banks then had in circulation. There had previously been no limit to the amount of credit-notes that a bank might issue, and the change was made not because of evil consequences that had arisen from this freedom, but in order to bring the Scotch banks under the restrictive rulings of the English banking law.

Evidence taken by a committee of the House of Commons in 1826 shows that during the whole period of note issue in Scotland (one hundred and twenty-two years) the loss sustained by the public on bank-notes had been only £36,344; while the losses in England on English bank-notes had been relatively very much greater. That the Scotch system was then a more efficient and better-working system than the English is evidenced by the testimony of numerous writers. Sir Walter Scott, writing on this subject in 1826, admonishes England not to impose her banking laws upon Scotland, and says, " But neglected as she was, and perhaps because she was neglected, Scotland, reckoning her progress during the space from the close of the American war to the present day, has increased her prosperity in a ratio more than five times greater than that of her more fortunate and richer sister."[1]

The Scotch people, fully realizing the great benefits derived from their system of free banking, resisted every move made by England to impose her system upon them. In order to overcome this opposition, Sir Robert Peel's Ministry resorted to a measure which was in the nature of a bribe, in that it permitted the Scotch banks to continue the issue of credit-notes to the extent of their circulation at the time, with the additional privilege of an unlimited issue of notes against gold, while to all banks of later origin the right of note issue was entirely denied. A monopoly of note issue in Scotland was thus created for banks then in existence.[2]

The second example of free banking referred to is found in Canada. In its essential features it is the Scotch system transplanted by Scotchmen to their new home. Though it has been modified from time

---

[1] Malachi Malagrowther on the *Proposed Change of Banking*, p. 10.
[2] For a complete exposition of the Scotch banking system, see *The Scotch Banks and System of Issue*, by Robt. Somers, Edinburgh, 1873.

to time, it has not been improved. It may be questioned whether Canada fully appreciates the great advantages of the Scotch system; if she did, the bankers would have more support in their struggle to preserve it in its integrity against the assaults made upon it whenever banking legislation comes up in Parliament. In ignorance of the evil effects of his acts, the Canadian politician has used his legislative power over the currency as an easy means of obtaining capital in a way which shall not impress the public as creating a new indebtedness. The distinctive functions of money and capital he does not perceive, hence to issue government paper money and to make it legal tender, and to create government savings-banks, are his special monetary achievements. He little suspects that legal-tender notes are weakness and not strength, and that by forcing these notes into the circulation he is paralyzing the industry of the Dominion. Every few years the volume of government paper money is enlarged. There are now $25,000,000 of it in the circulation, and to prevent its coming back upon the Government the banks are required to carry forty per cent. of their reserves in this paper. The first cost of this paper issue to the people of Canada is exactly $25,000,000 in gold or its equivalent, but what its ultimate cost will be is hardly computable. We may be certain, however, that it is all floating capital abstracted from the industries of the country, and dissipated. How long it will be before Canada shall be in the same monetary muddle as that in which the United States now finds itself, remains to be seen; if the politicians have their way, it will not be long. The official reports for the month of July, 1896, show the amount of deposits in the Canadian Government Post-Office and Savings Banks to be $47,017,282. Fortunately the United States is not afflicted with this paternal system of banking. A commercial savings-bank is a nursery of floating capital, a government savings-bank is a squanderer of floating capital.

The chief function of a bank is to utilize the capital of the industrial community in which it is situated, but this it cannot do to the fullest extent if debarred from the exercise of its natural right to use its credit in issuing notes. If it must use government notes only—their cost being exactly equal to their nominal value in gold money—the effective working capital of the bank is thereby reduced in amount, and the community generally is also prevented from utilizing its capital in effecting exchanges. Issuing notes is a normal business transaction between the bank and its customers, whereby the products of the community in their various stages of transition from the growing crop, or from the raw material, to the market, are largely utilized in the reproduction of capital. By employing these products (all of which are capital) as collateral security for the redemption of the notes in the precious metal selected by the community as its monetary standard, this metal is economized to the extent of about nine-tenths of what would otherwise be required, and the nine-tenths saved becomes producing capital. When a given sum of money is deposited in bank, the deposit is practically a transfer of capital from some other point to the bank, the money being the medium employed to effect the transfer.

Some economists assert that money is non-productive because it does nothing but effect exchanges, but this theory is misleading, for though money in itself is not directly productive, it is an agent whereby the productiveness of capital is immensely increased. The theory is further misleading in that it ignores the fact that all kinds of money do not equally stimulate the productiveness of capital. Bank-notes, for example, are more stimulative than government notes, and it is therefore proper to speak of bank-notes as more productive than government notes.

When a bank lends its notes to a farmer to enable him to bridge the period between the planting and the marketing of his crop, and the farmer transfers to the bank a legal claim upon the crop to the extent of his borrowing, this is a transfer of capital from the farmer to the bank in exchange for the notes. The farmer may use the notes to pay his field-hands, to buy a new implement or repair an old one, to pay his household expenses, or to do anything necessary to bring his crop to maturity and to sale; the service which the notes will have performed when he has spent them is the transfer in exchange for them of capital which appears in the matured crop.

In the strict sense, a bank is an integral part of an industrial community, and note issue is an integral part of banking. Deprive the bank of its natural right to issue credit-notes, and it is maimed; deprive the community of its banks, and the industrial organism is disrupted. The pecuniary liability of the community in the conduct of a bank exceeds in most cases that of the shareholders, and the relation of the banker to the community is in the nature of a trust. His position enables him to acquire a general and intimate knowledge of the activities of the community and of the business ability and trustworthiness of its members; and as the prosperity of the bank is dependent upon the prosperity of the community, the banker becomes, in a certain sense, a supervisor for the community in so far as relates to the money and capital employed.

We have seen that the issuance of credit-notes is a joint transaction of the bank with its customers, the bank on its part agreeing to maintain a sufficient reserve in coin to redeem the notes on demand, the bank and customers together pledging capital for the faithful fulfilment of the obligation; hence the gain, whatever it may be, properly belongs to the bank, its customers, and the community, and if not interfered with by the State, will be equitably distributed among them with the certainty of a natural law. Gain there is, but immediate profit in the form of capital there certainly is not; therefore to tax these notes is to obstruct and hinder productiveness. The notes are simply a means to an end; while in circulation they represent capital of a mixed character, but capital that has already been taxed or that is subject to taxation; when not in circulation, they have no value, nor do they represent value.

When, in 1892, the New York Stock Exchange adopted a clearing-house system, a saving of its members' time and a lessening of their risks were thereby effected — advantages in which the whole financial community to some extent participates; yet none will contend that the saving in this instance is of property, or that the mechanism employed to effect this saving should be taxed. The case is similar when an industrial community adopts a plan of note issue which at once reduces the cost and increases the efficiency of its medium of exchange, while at the same time it enlarges the productive power of the community. Why, then, should our Government interpose by the exercise of its taxing power to arrest this salutary movement? A vague and undefined apprehension that these notes may overspread the circulation to the exclusion of better money is all that prevents their use. The imperfections of our paper circulation prior to the Civil War, when it was composed exclusively of State-bank notes, are cited in advocacy of government notes; but if the banking laws of the different States, as they existed before the war, are examined, it will be found that they were not formulated in accordance with banking principles. It is therefore to the vicious charters under which State banks were organized that the bank failures and the currency panics must be ascribed.

A bank's dealings are in floating capital and money. What is known to the economist as floating capital is called by the merchant " quick assets," and may be any product of the farm, the mine, or the factory, in crop, in store, or in transit to market; or any other of the products of industry. The farm and buildings, the mine stripped of its portable machinery and tools, and the factory similarly stripped, are all fixed capital, and cannot be made productive without the aid of labor and of floating capital. It is this floating capital that gives direct effect to labor; work cannot proceed on the farm, in the mine, or in the factory without it, nor can such capital be made effective without a sufficiency of money. The productive power of a community is proportioned to the number of hands and the amount of floating capital employed. If the floating capital is insufficient, there will be idle hands that must seek work elsewhere; if it is superabundant, the surplus will be transferred to points where it can find profitable employment.

In a new country like ours, there is a constant tendency to convert floating into fixed capital, until the proportion of floating capital is insufficient to fully utilize the fixed capital. The prairie must be broken, mines opened, houses, roads, bridges, and mills must be built, all of which necessarily convert floating capital into fixed capital. Statistical tables show that the wealth of the United States and of England are nearly equal in amount, but there is a marked difference in the character of the assets. In England no fixed capital ever lies idle merely for the want of floating capital to make it productive, whereas in our country this condition is common. The immense natural resources of our country are a constant incitement to new industrial enterprises; and all such ventures, however wisely projected and carried out, necessarily convert into fixed capital much of the floating capital employed. There is also a great influx of foreign labor; statistics show that 4,560,729 immigrants have been added to our population within the last decade, which makes the need of a corresponding inflow of capital imperative.

Speaking of England's abundant floating capital, Walter Bagehot says: " We have entirely lost the idea that any undertaking likely to pay, and seen to be likely, can perish for want of money; yet no idea was more familiar to our ancestors, or is more common now in most countries."[1] Substitute the

[1] *Lombard Street* (ninth edition), p. 7. London, 1888.

words "floating capital" for the word "money" in the above quotation, and we shall have the strict meaning that the writer doubtless intended to convey. The words "money" and "capital," in the language of Lombard and Wall Streets, are by common usage synonymous terms, and are often so used even by those who fully discriminate between their differing application. But even among business men with whom the words "money" and "capital" are so commonly convertible terms, it is always floating and never fixed capital that the word "money" is made to overlap.

All the assets of a bank should be what is commonly called "quick assets," in other words, floating capital and money. Gold and silver, when not in service as money, are floating capital. As a bank must be at all times in position to meet its liabilities in current money and the larger part of them on demand, its assets cannot drift from floating into fixed capital without diminishing its banking capabilities and ultimately imperilling its existence. A bank may be, and generally is, the medium whereby floating capital is transferred from one point to another for conversion into fixed capital, but its own capital and the deposits of its customers must be preserved in the form of floating capital and money. A bank which should permit its floating capital and money to assume the form of fixed capital would be as completely out of banking business as a grocer who had bartered his stock in trade for a stone quarry would be out of the grocery business. The banker, or bank examiner, who cannot readily distinguish between floating and fixed capital is unfit for his position.

Under banking laws framed in accordance with correct banking principles, the deposits of a regularly conducted bank will naturally increase, but its note issue does not necessarily increase, for the notes are used only to effect exchanges, and the amount issued is consequently limited by the number and value of the exchanges to be effected. With free banking the limitations of expediency which naturally surround a bank will keep it within its legitimate sphere of action. The deposits are floating capital, and it is mainly from the deposits that a bank derives, or with such freedom would derive, its profits. This being the case, a bank cannot force its note issue without imperilling its credit; and to lose its credit is to lose its deposits. We must keep in mind that the larger part of the deposits, as well as all the notes, are payable on demand. The notes must have the confidence of the community in order to maintain their nominal value in the circulation, and even then their volume cannot be increased beyond the needs of the community, for those who keep the notes in circulation will no more hold capital in idleness than will the bank itself, and to hold notes that are not needed is to keep in idleness the capital which was parted with to obtain the notes.

As a bank's deposits are its chief source of profit, it is to the interest of the bank to increase them as far as possible; and as, to preserve the existence of the bank, these deposits must be held in the form of floating capital, the banker must keep a careful watch on the uses to which this capital is applied, and must lend assistance to no project which in his judgment would waste it, or lock it up as unproductive fixed capital. As the knowledge necessary to such wholesome supervision can be acquired only through personal business association, it follows that a banker's work lies mainly within the community of which his bank is an integral part, and that the interests of the bank and of the community are identical.

In support of the statement that the limitations of expediency which naturally surround a bank under a free banking system will keep it within its legitimate sphere of action, there is here given the ratio of note issue to deposits of the Bank of Dundee, Scotland, between the years 1784 and 1844. It will be remembered that in 1765 the Scotch banks were prohibited from issuing any notes that were not payable in the metallic standard on demand, and that it was not until 1845 that any limit was placed upon the amount of notes that a bank might issue. It should be noted that the Bank of Dundee began business in 1764 upon a basis of money-lending and note issue only, and did not become a bank of deposit until 1792. The figures compared are taken at intervals of ten years.

YEAR.	NOTE ISSUE.	DEPOSITS.
1784	£56,342	None
1794	50,254	£48,809
1804	54,096	157,821
1814	46,627	445,066
1824	29,675	343,948
1834	26,467	563,202
1844	27,504	535,253

The experience of the Bank of Dundee in regard to its note issue and deposits was not exceptional, but is in accord with the general experience of the Scotch banks during the period mentioned. The Scotch banker of 1764-84 was doubtless infected with the belief, still so commonly entertained, that there existed a hidden mine of wealth which might be worked by the simple and inexpensive process of issuing notes. All that was needed to dispel this delusion was freedom to work the imaginary mine at will, and his every-day experience in practical banking eventually taught the Scotch banker that his larger interests were best served by such co-operation with his customers as would increase their prosperity. The only lines upon which banking can advance have been fixed by natural laws which neither the banker nor the customer can infringe with impunity.

We have seen that in order to fulfil its functions efficiently, paper money should be local money, and that to be so, it must be bank-notes payable on demand in metallic money at the counter of the bank of issue. We have also seen that a bank in its entirety is an integral part of an industrial community, and that the community's pecuniary interest in the bank is generally greater than that of the shareholders. These essential principles indicate unmistakably what a government may and may not do, legislatively, in the interest of sound and serviceable banking. By the issuance of a note, a bank contracts to pay to bearer on demand a given amount of precious metal; it therefore becomes a function of government, on default of such payment by the bank, to enforce the contract. It is also properly a function of government, in granting bank charters, to provide that the business of the bank shall be conducted with such openness as shall keep the public informed as to its financial condition. Beyond these essential provisions, there is little or nothing that a government can do in banking legislation to protect the interests of the public. To require a bank to keep a specific amount of money constantly in reserve can have no effect but to obstruct the working of the bank; to require a bonded security on the notes issued is destructive of their efficiency.

Our Government's present system of bank auditing is essentially defective. The published statements do not convey the information necessary to enable the interested public to form an intelligent judgment of a bank's condition, and the examiners themselves, in too many instances, are not qualified for their duties. Of this we have ample proof in the exhibits of assets and liabilities made by banks that have failed. These exhibits frequently furnish conclusive evidence of ignorant or dishonest bank management, long continued, which was made possible only through the defective statements of the bank examiners. Irregularities in banking should be immediately exposed, the examiner not being allowed any discretion on this point. In a bank statement the quick assets should always be presented distinct and apart from assets that are not readily convertible, hence an intimate knowledge of the character and value of the assets examined is necessary to a correct audit. An experienced banker will detect irregularities in banking from signs and indications that would be altogether overlooked by the uninitiated. It would be well for our Government to delegate to the clearing-houses the appointment of bank examiners. These organizations embody the best banking talent of the country, and they are directly interested in the maintenance of sound banking.

It is claimed by some that it would be advantageous for the United States to change the present system of individual banks for a system of parent banks with numerous branches, such as exists in England and in Canada. It may be well, therefore, to briefly indicate the distinctive features of the two systems. The parent system is monopolistic in its nature, inasmuch as it reduces the number of banks competing greatly below the total number of banks. So far as the customer is concerned, he gains no advantage from the parent system; if he opens an account with a branch bank, his dealings are as exclusively with that branch as if it stood alone. In the matter of note issue, the notes are paid out at all of the branches, while the obligation to redeem them is confined to the counter of the parent bank. Deposits kept at the parent bank cannot be checked upon through any of the branches.[1]

It may seem at first sight that the parent system has greater strength than our individual system, but the contrary is really the case. This apparent strength is the result of a common but erroneous belief that the floating capital of the nation is owned by capitalists, corporate banks, and individual bankers; and this belief has impressed the people with a sense of dependence upon capitalists and banks. The fact is that the available working capital, in other words, the floating capital of the nation, really belongs chiefly to the large class of persons of small or moderate means, and the banks and bankers are simply its administrators.

The following data, taken from the Report of the United States Comptroller of the Currency for 1895, show that the liabilities to depositors and note-hold-

---

[1] The Bank of England issues notes from its branch banks, which are redeemable either at the parent bank or at the bank of issue.

ers of 9815 National and other banks were $5,082,-922,280, while the total capital of these banks, together with their surplus reserves, amounted to $1,786,473,471. This shows that the capital of the shareholders amounted to one quarter of the total capital administered by the banks. The report does not give the average amount due to each depositor in the commercial banks, but the average per capita for the savings-banks is given as being $371.36, and the total deposits of the savings-banks (included in the total deposits of all banks as already given) were $1,810,507,023. On the whole, we may reasonably conclude from these data, that fully four fifths of the total floating capital of the nation is the property of the great body of people of moderate means.

A serious objection to the parent system is that it has a tendency to draw the floating capital of the country to the commercial centres where the parent banks are located. This tendency results naturally from the fact that all the branches of each parent bank are under the absolute control of the board of managers of the central bank. However great the banking capabilities of this board may be, it cannot know the standing of the customers of the branch banks, and the needs of the districts in which those banks are situated, as well as it knows the customers and the district over which it has itself direct personal supervision. Inasmuch as the chief aim of the managers of a bank is to make dividends, they naturally direct their energies into those channels which promise the largest returns in dividends. It is also the case that in making loans they will prefer those loans over which they can keep direct supervision. As at the commercial centres money can generally be safely and profitably lent to persons engaged in speculative ventures, such loans are frequently made, with the result that much of the capital controlled by these banks is diverted from points where it might be used productively into non-productive employment at these centres.

On the other hand, in independent banking the bank-owners and the customers are brought into direct contact, an advantage, as compared with dealing with an intermediary, which every business man can appreciate. These bankers being in position, from personal association and observation, to form a competent judgment of the industrial enterprises of their customers, banks and customers are thus brought into closer co-operative union. Moreover, as the prosperity of a bank and its customers is largely dependent upon the amount of floating capital employed, every independent bank becomes a competitor for this form of capital, and the tendency of this competition is to diffuse the floating capital of the country instead of concentrating it at the commercial centres. When the need arises for a combination of banks under a system of independent banking, there naturally develops the organization of clearing-house associations. Through these associations the highest degree of strength is attained without impairing the democratic character of the system.

All banks come into existence and are governed in their business by individual self-interest; they cannot be run on altruistic principles. If our banks and their customers are debarred from using their capital and credit to create their medium of exchange, and are obliged to use government notes instead, it cannot be expected that banks should keep such a supply of this costly money always on hand as will meet the legitimate demands of all their customers at all times. Many of these customers will therefore often be compelled to labor without money, their industries languishing in consequence. Redundant money in the city of New York does not help the Alabama planter and the Nebraska farmer to harvest their crops; and to tell these people that they can have the money they so much need if they will " put up the requisite collateral," is to mock them in their extremity. In a new country like ours, with its immense productive possibilities, two per cent. per annum for money in New York means congestion, and from eight to forty per cent. in the Southern and Western States means paralysis.

CHAPTER IV.

ARGUMENTS IN SUPPORT OF THE PROPOSED LEGISLATIVE CHANGES.

AMONG the legislative changes here proposed with the object of bringing our monetary system into accord with monetary principles, is one requiring that the holder of any United States money brought to the Treasury shall have the right to have it exchanged for any other United States money he may wish. This proposition necessarily includes the three following propositions: first, that the Secretary of the Treasury shall be authorized to retain in the Treasury and retire from circulation any kind of money that the people reject; second, that he shall be empowered to issue and sell bonds when in his judgment such sales are necessary to enable him to meet any demands on the Treasury which may result from these changes; third, that to the buyers of these bonds shall be granted the right to pay for them in any money of the United States, either gold, silver, or paper. As the people in their dealings with one another are now required to accept these different kinds of money at a parity of value, it is only consistent that the Government itself should so accept them. For a government arbitrarily to discriminate between its different issues of money is to discredit the issue discriminated against, and to raise a doubt as to the good faith of the government itself. A public sense of security is a primary requisite of all industrial progress.

Our currency should be both stable and efficient, and to be so it must be self-regulative. Stability there cannot be unless the coins take their value from the bullion market, and this implies entire freedom on the part of the individual to have his bullion coined, to buy and sell the precious metals, coined or uncoined, to export and import them, coined or uncoined; it implies also that no attempt shall be made by the State to give to the coins a factitious current value. If, then, it were made imperative that the issuers of paper money should redeem their notes on demand in coin of the metal which the notes represent, our whole currency would become self-regulative, and could only rise and fall in value with the rise and fall of bullion in the market of the world. This is the highest degree of stability which currency can acquire.

Under these free conditions, silver and gold coin would be independent of each other, and would have an equal chance to prove their respective merits. As all the different issues of paper money would be on an equal footing, these issues must also establish their fitness for the special service required of them. It would then be seen that money is no exception to that universal law which declares that the inferior implement is displaced by one of superior efficiency. The money best adapted to a particular service would be the money selected for that service, and through this process of individual selection our currency would ultimately acquire the highest possible efficiency.

There could then be no inflation of the currency. If the issues of bank-notes in the different localities increased the volume beyond the needs of the nation at large, government notes would be brought to the Treasury for redemption in metallic money; if this metallic money were not needed, it would either be appropriated for use in the arts or exported.

As the people have long been accustomed to government notes, and as these notes have come to be generally regarded as the best form of paper money, they will not be driven from the circulation unless they are manifestly inefficient. Starting with the popular prepossession in their favor, government notes would hold their place in the circulation at every point where their service could be made available.

Here arises a question as to whether government notes of the denominations below five dollars would not continue to circulate indefinitely. One- and two-dollar notes are so largely used for pocket-money, and the need for them is so positive and continuous, that they are rarely returned to the Treasury for redemption until they are too much worn for further service, and their remaining out so long seriously lessens their usefulness as a medium for imparting elasticity to the currency. It is commonly supposed that because our currency is now so exclusively paper, paper it will continue to be; but this is a gratuitous assumption. Individually the people have had no choice in the selection of their money. To what extent coin would come into general use as pocket-money under better monetary conditions remains an open question.

It has already been stated that the normal relative proportion of paper to metallic money under a system of individual banking would be about nine of paper to one of metal, but this statement applies only to the Eastern and Middle States. As in all of the Southern States silver would certainly be adopted as the monetary standard, it may safely be predicted that in those States the proportion of metallic money in the circulation would be greater than that of paper. The negro cannot by any artifice or magic be lifted at once into the sphere of industrial civilization that, in the development of credit as a monetary factor, it has taken the Anglo-Saxon two hundred years to attain. Banks are as yet a mystery to the negro, and paper money he will not take if he can as readily obtain silver. He must be allowed time to work his way through the intricacies of finance as the white man has done before him. If he is let alone, his first step in acquiring habits of thrift will be to hoard his savings in silver dollars, and as a hoarder he will become a conservator of the State. Silver is the money of his choice, and the duty of the State towards him is to see that this money is not the false dollars that he must now accept, but that their intrinsic is equal to their nominal value.

The adoption of the monetary reform here proposed would require the Secretary of the Treasury, in the progress of that reform, to exercise such of the functions of a banker as are not incompatible with his fiscal duties. The banker pays out and takes in money in accordance with the requirements of his customers, and the Secretary would deal in the same way with persons coming to the Treasury. During the past thirty-five years a series of Acts have been passed which required the exercise of banking functions by the Secretary of the Treasury, while at the same time the power to execute them has been withheld or denied. Whatever reform of the currency may be instituted, these powers must be granted in order to avoid the risk of involving the country in financial embarrassment during the period of transition. The Secretary must be free to pay out money, to take it in, and to exchange one kind of money for another, this being the only means whereby elasticity can be imparted to the currency until such time as it becomes self-regulative through individual action. The able management of the Treasury Department through the many difficulties that have arisen from defective legislation is a guaranty that any larger power granted to the Secretary would be judiciously exercised. To pledge the nation to the payment of its bonded indebtedness in gold money, and to give to individuals the option of exchanging any United States money they may hold for any other United States money, would at once restore public confidence, and bring gold into the circulation. The Mint Report for 1896 gives $625,047,484 as the amount of gold coin in the United States November 1, 1896. Why, then, should there be so much difficulty in maintaining a sufficient gold reserve in the Treasury? No reason can be assigned but the uncertainty as to the legal interpretation of the various Acts under which United States money has been issued. If, as is claimed by some, greenbacks and Treasury notes are payable in gold, these notes should be held with the same sense of security as gold certificates; but they are not so held. A promise is as binding in the one case as in the other, and no one can doubt either the ability or the disposition of the United States to fulfil a promise once made. The fact is that greenbacks and Treasury notes are now payable in gold rather by implication than by direct agreement.

The outstanding obligations of the Government should be payable in gold money for the reason that they were contracted under that standard. The greenback indebtedness was not specifically so contracted, yet the obligation to redeem them also in gold is equally binding, because all of the present holders have accepted them under that standard. As money is simply a commodity selected by a people to enable them to effect their exchanges with greater facility than could be done under a system of barter, a plea cannot rightfully be set up that because the commodity selected has meanwhile changed in value, there is no longer any obligation to make payment as agreed, and that it may be done in another commodity. When a commodity is adopted to serve as money, it is the specific article and not a specific value that is adopted. All commodities are constantly changing their value in relation to one another; a specifically fixed value is therefore an impossibility. Allowing that Senator Jones is right in his opinion that the demonetization of silver has greatly advanced the value of gold, this condition does not lessen the binding force of the obligation to settle in gold money all transactions made during the continuance of that standard.

A law which is inherently defective, and which besides is rendered absolutely inoperative by other legislation and by executive acts of the Government, is practically a dead letter. This is the case with the Bland Act, passed February 28, 1878. The members of Congress who secured the passage of this Act doubtless supposed that they were creating a silver standard; but if it is now found that they were mistaken, and that no silver standard was thereby created, the nation as a whole is in justice bound to assume the losses occasioned by the mistake of its representatives, and must not leave it to circumstance to decide who shall be the individual victims of that mistake.

A brief recapitulation of monetary principles as applied to legislation will show that the opposing parties in the conflict of the standards are all more or less responsible for our present difficulties. The Act of February 12, 1873, which demonetized silver, was passed under the impression that a single metal should constitute the monetary standard of a nation, and in selecting gold as this standard, the framers of the Act doubtless believed that gold was the metal best adapted to our use. They simply acted upon the gold monometallic theory. Except during the years between 1873 and 1878, our monetary laws have been framed upon the bimetallic theory, with the result that silver money was our only standard down to 1834, and from that date to the present time gold alone has been the standard, except when the country was on the basis of an inconvertible paper money.

When the Act of February 12, 1873, was passed, the country was on a paper basis; consequently, although this Act demonetized silver, it did not expel any silver money from the circulation, for that had already been done by the Act of June 28, 1834, which fixed the ratio at sixteen of silver to one of gold. There was no time from the passage of that Act until 1874 that sixteen ounces of silver bullion had not a greater purchasing power in the markets of the world than one ounce of gold bullion had; it was consequently the Act of 1834 that constituted gold as the standard and deposed silver. This was the natural result of bimetallic legislation.

The Acts of February 28, 1878, and July 14, 1890, have had the effect of putting into circulation about fifty million silver dollars, which, however, are not silver money. As these dollars may readily be exchanged for gold, they pass current at the gold-standard valuation; they therefore represent gold money in the circulation in the same way that paper represents it. As the metals constitute basic money they may be represented in the circulation by paper, but to make one metal represent the other is to deprive the representing metal of its monetary function as a measure of value, and to reduce it to subsidiary service as a medium of exchange.

If, then, the silver dollars in circulation serve only as a medium of exchange, what service is performed by the $496,000,000 in silver lying in the vaults of the Treasury? It may be said that they are represented in the circulation by silver certificates, but as these certificates are as readily convertible into gold as are the silver dollars in circulation, the certificates also pass current at the gold-standard valuation, and therefore must also represent gold money. If the silver dollars in the Treasury vaults are needed as a collateral security to support the credit of the United States, and so to ensure the redemption of the silver certificates in gold money, they are floating capital in that service; if they are not so needed, they perform no service whatever. This being so, it necessarily follows that our silver legislation has not only failed to give us silver money, but has discredited silver. The steady accumulation of silver in the Treasury vaults between 1878 and 1890 was watched by the whole financial world with growing apprehension that this silver might at any time be precipitated upon the bullion market, and it still remains a menace to that market.

That our silver legislation has miscarried is the inevitable outcome of the erroneous ideas in reference to money which enter into and dominate our monetary laws. No distinction is made between money and capital. The monetary needs of the nation are computed as per capita; the great importance of credit as a factor in economizing capital and promoting prosperity is overlooked, and the long-established fundamental principle that money is a commodity is obscured by the idea that the coin acquires its value from the stamp. In the Senate of the United States the theory has been propounded that "value does not reside in the material, but in the stamp; in other words, on the legal tender impressed on that material."[1] If that be so, how comes it that the precious metals were fulfilling the function of money long before people had thought of either stamping or coining the metal? The fact is, that down to the time of Queen Elizabeth, the English people continued the practice of weighing their silver money, whether coined or uncoined; the stamp on the coin had no significance to them but that it guaranteed the fineness of the metal.[2]

[1] Speech of Senator John P. Jones, delivered May 12 and 13, 1890, p. 65.
[2] *The Economic Interpretation of History*, by J. E. T. Rogers, chap. ix.

CHAPTER V.

THE PRECIOUS METALS AS AFFECTED IN THEIR RELATIVE VALUE BY PRODUCTION AND BY DEMONETIZATION.

FOR seventy years prior to 1871, in which year Germany demonetized silver, the limits of variation in the relative market value of the precious metals were 15.04 to 1, and 16.25 to 1; whereas in the twenty-three years following 1871, the ratio changed from 15.57 to 1 to 32.56 to 1. There are two ways in which this great disparity in relative value may be accounted for: First, by a reduction in the cost of producing one of the metals, with no corresponding reduction in the cost of producing the other; second, by a relatively greater increase in the demand for one, or what is substantially the same, by the closing against the other of markets which it had previously filled. A permanent reduction in the cost of producing one of the metals, with no corresponding reduction in the cost of producing the other, would create a permanent change in the relative value of the two metals; but if the disparity we are now considering had resulted from this cause alone, the change would have taken place more slowly, because great stability is a distinguishing feature of bullion as compared with other commodities.

All other commodities lack in a greater or less degree the elements which combine to give stability in value to the precious metals. Of these elements, a wide market is of first importance; durability and easy portability also contribute to steadiness of value. When two commodities are adapted to similar uses, so that one may be substituted for the other, an element of steadiness in value is thereby imparted to them. While the precious metals possess all these elements in a high degree, the fact that they alone are universally used as money gives them an added stability over all other commodities. Employed as the measure of value, their fluctuations in value are unsuspected; they consequently yield slowly to the influence of supply and demand. And as they are the only metals having an extended market which can be coined into suitably sized pieces for handling and expressing value, there is nothing that can supersede them. Their use as money carries them all over the globe and (even as bullion) renders them everywhere more readily convertible into other property than any other commodity. This ready exchangeability, with their easy portability, practically brings the silver and gold of the world into one great market—the bullion market.

The late Dr. Adolphe Soetbeer, of Göttingen, in his *Materials towards the Elucidation of the Economic Conditions Affecting the Precious Metals*, has furnished the most complete collection of facts and figures that now exists, illustrative of the changes that have taken place in the production, consumption, and values of these metals, and in prices generally. Professor Soetbeer had unrestricted opportunities for reference and research, and his work is accepted as of the highest authority. His figures are the best we have from attainable data for the period covered by his work.

The following table, made up from figures of Professor Soetbeer, shows the world's average annual product of gold and silver for the periods named:

PERIOD.	GOLD OUNCES.	SILVER OUNCES.
1801–1840	512,214	20,028,887
1841–1850	1,760,502	25,090,342
1851–1870	6,279,063	34,009,395 [1]

[1] The reader will find at the end of the book a more extended table showing the relative production of silver and gold; also a table showing the relative value of these metals between the years 1661 and 1885.

The following additional figures are taken, and the deductions drawn, from Professor Soetbeer's tables, and from tables compiled by John S. Hanson, and published in pamphlet form, in 1896, by the Fourth National Bank of the City of New York.

After 1870 the production of gold declined and remained almost stationary until 1890, when it began to increase. The production of gold in 1894 was double that of 1874. The annual production of gold is now (1897) estimated at 10,000,000 ounces, and is rapidly increasing.

The production of silver in 1870 was 46,800,000 ounces, and there was a continuous and rapid annual increase until 1894, when it had reached 167,753,-000 ounces.

The average annual production of gold in the twenty years from 1851 to 1870 was eleven hundred and twenty-five per cent. greater than it had been for the forty years prior to 1841, while during the same period the average annual production of silver increased only seventy per cent. This great increase in the production of gold was caused by the discovery of gold in California and in Australia, which occurred respectively in 1849 and 1851.

The production of silver in 1894 was three hundred and ninety-three per cent. greater than the annual average from 1851 to 1870; while the production of gold in 1894 was an increase of only thirty-nine per cent. over the annual average from 1851 to 1870.

The production of silver in 1894 was seven hundred and thirty-eight per cent. greater than the annual average of the forty years prior to 1841, while the production of gold in 1894 was sixteen hundred and six per cent. greater than the annual average of the forty years prior to 1841.

The above figures and comparisons show that for the twenty years from 1851 to 1870, there was a great increase in the production of gold, and that for the twenty years from 1871 to 1890, there was a great increase in the production of silver; they also show that the increase in the production of gold has been on the whole more than double that of silver, as compared with their relative production for the forty years from 1801 to 1841.

It will be seen, then, that the figures of production lend no support to the belief so commonly entertained that the disparity in the relative value of the two metals, which began to be manifest in 1873, was caused by an over-production of silver.

The increase in the production of gold in the twenty years previous to 1870 was relatively double that of silver in the subsequent twenty years, yet the relative value of the two metals in the first twenty years named was only fractionally disturbed, while in the second twenty years that relative value changed from 15.57 to 1 to 19.76 to 1, and there was thereafter a continually increasing disparity, which in 1894 had reached 32.56 to 1.

If, from 1871 to 1890, when silver was so largely produced, the bullion market had been as free from artificial interferences as it was from 1851 to 1870, when gold was so largely produced, it can hardly be questioned that the relative value of the metals would have been as little disturbed by the overflow of silver as it had been by the overflow of gold. Nor is it reasonable to suppose that the introduction of cheaper methods of producing silver could have acted so promptly and directly upon the bullion market, if there had been no other cause for the change in the relative value of the two metals. But no competent authority claims that there has been any special cheapening of the cost of producing silver since 1870. Improvements in transportation, in machinery, and in tools are not peculiar to silver-mining, but are equally applicable in gold-mining and in the production of nearly all other commodities.

A discovery of a rich deposit of silver is no more

likely than a discovery of a rich deposit of gold; indeed, geologists and mineralogists say that the chance of a rich find is more likely to be of gold than of silver, and the evidence of the nineteenth century, set forth in the figures before us, sustains this view.

By 1892 the rapid increase in the production of silver had ceased, while since that date the production of gold has been, and still is, rapidly rising. At present the yield of silver by weight is not sixteen times greater than that of gold. On the whole it must be admitted that the figures of production flatly contradict the claim so frequently made, that the present disparity in the relative value of the two metals is caused by the over-production of silver. It is impossible to avoid the conclusion that it is the demonetization of silver, and not its over-production, that is the chief cause of the disparity in value.

A fact to be noted is that a lack of uniformity in the production of the precious metals has been its characteristic feature from the earliest times. At irregular intervals the production of one metal has greatly exceeded that of the other; yet, from the sixteenth century, when the cost of producing silver was greatly reduced by the invention of the process of amalgamation, down to the time when the silver demonetizing movement began (1871), this disparity in production had not materially affected the relative value of the two metals in the open market of the world. Another fact to be noted is that, until the demonetizing movement began, long-continued and wide-spread industrial prosperity followed every extraordinary increase in the supply of either or both of these metals. This was the experience of Europe upon the influx of these metals from America after the Spanish conquest; it was also the experience of the world generally after the discovery of gold in California and Australia.

It is unnecessary to say that, under normal conditions, there is no better way of ascertaining whether there has been a rise or a fall in the value of metallic money than by comparing its purchasing power at different periods; the conditions, however, are not now normal. In the past twenty-five years the interferences with metallic money, and consequently with the bullion market, have been of the most arbitrary character, and on a scale of greater magnitude than at any previous time. Under normal conditions the money metals are the most stable of all commodities. It is for this reason chiefly that they have come to be employed to measure the value of other commodities; but even under normal conditions, so long as we must use a commodity as the measure, we cannot have a fixed standard, though we may have a reasonably steady one. To maintain a uniform and fixed value for the money metals, their volume would have to bear a continuously uniform proportion to the volume of commodities, properties, and services to be measured.

The advocates of gold monometallism assume that gold is naturally more stable in value than silver, but this is a question upon which economists are about equally divided; it is, moreover, a purely speculative question which cannot be definitely determined. Value expresses the relation of all commodities to one another. It is not an inherent fixed quality in any commodity. Price expresses the relation of all commodities to the one commodity which has been selected by a community as its money. A rise in the price of silver bullion in New York is a fall in the price of gold bullion in Mexico, gold being the standard of value in New York and silver the standard of value in Mexico; but whether silver has risen or gold fallen, remains an open question. One or the other has certainly taken place, possibly both; but that is all we know about it.

The method employed to detect changes in the value of money relatively to other commodities is to note at stated intervals the price of a given number of staple commodities. If upon an average these prices rise, and the rise is maintained for a considerable length of time, it may be assumed that money has fallen in value. There are, however, so many factors which contribute to influence prices, that any conclusion reached even by this method can only be approximately correct.

It is a fundamental and accepted principle of economics that the cost of producing a commodity fixes what may properly be termed its normal value; but as cost itself varies from time to time, this normal value varies with it. For a time, in particular localities, supply and demand may run the price of a commodity greatly above or below its normal value. A "corner" in wheat in Chicago, or a famine in India, may advance the price of wheat abnormally in all the markets of the world, but such advance can be only temporary. The general trend of values of all staple commodities is towards the cost of production, including a small margin of profit.

We may be sure that the value of both metals changes in relation to one another and to all other commodities, but no evidence has yet been adduced to show that one naturally possesses any advantage in stability over the other. All the arguments advanced in proof of the greater stability of gold can easily be shown to be unsound. On the other hand, Dr. Soetbeer's tables furnish trustworthy evidence that the relative value of the two metals varied but little for more than two hundred years prior to 1871, which demonstrates that, with a free bullion market, both metals possess great stability, though it does not decide whether either is preferable in this respect. It is evident that the normal values of silver and of gold, as fixed by the cost of production, bear a definite relation to one another; and that with a free bullion market this relation would be preserved very closely, is a natural sequence. The conditions of a free bullion market are in the highest degree favorable to the maintenance of stability, and the fact that their uses are so largely the same that in most cases one may be substituted for the other, has undoubtedly contributed to overcome the extreme fluctuations in production and maintain steadiness in the value of both metals. That a great change in the relative value of these metals has taken place since 1871 is manifest, and that this change is a result of the demonetization of silver is a most reasonable hypothesis, but that one metal has remained stationary and the other alone has changed in value is a proposition that is not supported either by statistics or by logical deduction. The reasonable assumption is that gold has advanced and that silver has declined in value.

CHAPTER VI.

ON THE STANDARD OF VALUE.

PREVIOUS to the year 1867 the subject of monetary standards had not attracted public attention. In that year, upon the invitation of the French government, a conference was held in Paris to discuss and formulate a plan which should secure uniformity of coinage for the different nations; and it was this conference that brought the question of standards prominently before the world. For over two hundred years the two money metals had held such a uniform relative value that the possibility of disturbing it did not occur to any one; the business of the Convention was simply to select a monetary unit which should bring the currencies into such harmony that when prices were quoted in one country of the combination, they would be readily understood in another.

A *monetary standard*, or *standard of value*, is the

precious metal selected by a people to serve as their money; a *monetary unit*, or *unit of account*, is that coin which is their common denominator, and which contains a legally prescribed number of grains of the metal selected as their standard of value. Among commercial nations there are only two monetary standards, namely, silver and gold; but almost every nation has its own monetary unit, that of the United States being the dollar, that of France the franc, that of England the sovereign, etc. If we may judge from the practice of the past, it would seem that the aim of each nation, in making its monetary unit, had been to avoid uniformity with the unit of any other nation, and the result has undoubtedly operated as a bar to commercial intercourse between nations.

If our silver dollar passed at its market value as it should, and as it would under free coinage, and if this dollar contained exactly the same number of grains of silver as the Mexican dollar, can there be any doubt that the equality of value in these dollars would contribute to increase our trade, not only with Mexico, but with all those countries in which the Mexican dollar is current money? The silver dollar is current money in many of the South American States, along the coast of Eastern Asia, and in many parts of Africa; yet we have demonetized it, and our merchants are now computing their exchanges with those countries in pounds sterling.

The true solution of the problem before the Paris Convention was the adoption of two independent monetary units, one of silver and one of gold, each country being left free to choose its standard of value. By this action the number of monetary units would conform to the number of standards of value, which is the natural limit; with a free bullion market these units would acquire such a steady relative value as would give the nearest obtainable approach to a universal unit. Such a solution, however, could not have been entertained by a body, each member of which believed that only through the action of the State, and not by any natural process, could the coinage be regulated in these particulars.

Under these circumstances the first question for the decision of the Convention naturally was which metal should be selected as the monetary unit. The report of the Convention states that twenty countries were represented, and that only two of them had the gold standard. France wanted the unit to be of silver, but the English delegates had been instructed not to commit themselves to any unit that was not of gold, and England's preponderating influence in the commercial world seems to have prevailed, for the final decision of the Convention was for gold. There then followed *pour-parlers* between the different governments with the view of carrying out the decision arrived at. Nothing more could be done until France and England should come to an agreement. We have the statement of the British Chancellor of the Exchequer, made in 1869, that at that time " France was favorable to the abandonment of her silver standard "[1]; but the breaking out of the Franco-German war in the following year, and the result of that war, compelled France to suspend specie payment, and left Germany in a position to make the first move in demonetizing silver.

At that time the different monetary systems of the world were classified about as follows:

(1) England, Portugal, and Australia were gold monometallic.

(2) France, Belgium, Switzerland, Spain, New Granada, Chili, Peru, and Ecuador were bimetallic.

(3) Germany, Holland, Sweden, Norway, Denmark, Mexico, Central America, India, and China (commercially) were silver monometallic.

(4) United States, Brazil, Russia, Austria, Italy,

---

[1] *The Silver Question and the Gold Question*, by Robert Barclay, p. 122. London, 1885.

Turkey, and Greece were on an inconvertible paper basis.

It will be seen that of the nations that were upon a metallic basis, the money of groups 1 and 3 offset each other, while the money of group 2 changed from one metal to the other with the changes in the relative market value of the two metals. When the demonetization movement began, in 1871, the production of gold was declining and that of silver rapidly increasing, but if we consider that monetary legislation prior to that time had so little obstructed the natural play of the bullion market that even the great influx of gold from California and Australia did not seriously affect the relative value of the two metals, we must admit the most reasonable hypothesis to be that demonetization was the immediate and direct occasion of the rapid change which took place in that relative value after 1873. This demonetizing movement, begun by Germany in 1871, has continued to the present time, one nation after another falling into line. In 1873, Denmark, Sweden, and Norway adopted the gold standard both by law and in practice; in the same year France, Belgium, and Holland closed their mints against coining silver for individuals, but made no other change in their monetary laws. Other nations have since adopted the gold standard by statute, but have not yet been able to adopt it in practice. It is useless to recount all the monetary changes made by different nations since 1871; suffice to say that the mischievous movement to place the world upon an artificial monetary basis still goes on.

In order to appreciate why the relative market value of the two metals varied so little during the period from 1803 to 1873, we must exclude from our minds the commonly accepted idea that the Bank of France performed some special service with the express object of maintaining such uniformity. From this erroneous idea originate the proposals for a combination of the chief commercial nations to establish artificially a universal relative value for the precious metals. It is undoubtedly true that the Bank of France had great influence in preserving a uniform relative value throughout the whole period mentioned; but this influence was due to the fact that the bank made no effort whatever to preserve the legal ratio of fifteen and a half to one, and to the additional fact that the volume of precious metals in France exceeded their volume in any other European country, which made the French market the largest and consequently the controlling market for these metals. The practice of the Bank of

France in its dealings with its customers was to give them the choice of metals only when the legal and the market ratios were nearly in accord; in every instance where there was sufficient disparity to afford a profit, the bank took that profit by charging a premium on the coin of higher value, and this practice left both metals free to take their value from the bullion market.

The wealth of France in the precious metals is so largely a hoarded wealth that the total sum is not ascertainable. We caught a glimpse of this wealth in 1870 when the war indemnity of one thousand million dollars had to be paid to Germany. The Bank of France had previously suspended specie payments, and the nation's financial resources seemed for the time to be exhausted, yet the great sum was paid with a promptitude that astonished the financial world. Long exposure to frequent outbreaks of war has so far impressed the French mind with a sense of insecurity that it has retarded the nation's progress on the lines of commerce. In this respect England and France among advanced commercial nations represent the two extremes, the people of England utilizing their metallic money to a great extent through the use of credit, while the people of France still largely hoard theirs, as is shown by the fact that the private deposits in the Bank of France amount to only about one sixth of its note circulation. In further evidence it may be stated that the Bank of France is legally bound to establish a branch bank in every one of the eighty-six departments into which the country is divided, yet the people of France are so indifferent to banking privileges that to this day they have not required the entire fulfilment of this obligation, some eight or ten of these departments being still without a branch bank.

The formation in 1865 by France, Belgium, Switzerland, and Italy, of what is termed the Latin Union, did not have for its object the maintenance of a given ratio of value for the precious metals, as is commonly supposed. These nations, having previously adopted the ratio of fifteen and a half to one as an equivalent legal tender for their coins, had without specific agreement been acting with unanimity, and at their conference in 1865 it was incidentally agreed that their standard coins should thereafter be of uniform denomination and value, and that each nation should accept at its public treasury the coins of the other without distinction when of full weight. The monetary standard of these nations had been silver to 1850, but in the intervening fifteen years silver had gradually retired from the circulation, gold taking its place, in consequence of the relative cheapening of that metal caused by the great output of California and Australia. As their minor coinage was proportionately equal in value to the standard silver money, this minor coinage was also rapidly disappearing from circulation, thereby causing a great dearth of change-money. It was therefore in order to furnish and maintain a sufficient supply of fractional silver, and to make it uniform and interchangeable, that the convention was called which resolved itself into the Latin Union. To this end it was agreed (1st) to lower the value of the two-franc, one-franc, half-franc, and twenty-centime pieces by debasing the fineness of the silver from 0.900 to 0.835; (2d) that each nation should limit its coinage of these pieces to six francs per capita; (3d) that these coins should be accepted at the public treasury of each nation in sums not exceeding one hundred francs in one payment; (4th) that they should be a legal tender in the country where coined in sums not above fifty francs in one payment.

So long as silver continued to be relatively the more valuable metal, nothing was done by the Latin Union that could have the effect of restricting the freedom of the bullion market, but when silver became the cheaper metal, measures were adopted first to limit the coinage of five-franc silver pieces, and finally (1876) to suspend their coinage for individual account, thus placing the nations composing this Union practically upon the gold-standard basis. Germany had begun selling her demonetized silver in 1873, and her total sales, continued through five or six years, amounted to $300,000,000; this fact, together with the great increase in the production of silver at the time, and the discredit thrown upon this metal by the action of Germany, had alarmed the Latin Union, and had led it practically to demonetize silver.

In the world's mechanism of exchanges the Bank of France had for seventy years (from the granting of its charter in 1803) been the great balance-wheel in preserving uniformity in the relative value of the precious metals; but that this uniformity was the result of the bank's non-interference with the freedom of the bullion market, and not a consequence of the legal ratio adopted by the government of France, is further evidenced by Dr. Soetbeer's tables, which show that for one hundred and forty years prior to the incorporation of the Bank of France, the relative value of the two metals had been maintained as uniformly as during the bank's existence from 1803 to 1873.

For a long time prior to the adoption of gold monometallism by England, all of the commercial nations had been practically upon a silver-money basis, but this did not prevent gold from coming into monetary service wherever needed. It is true that there were interferences by which gold was frequently driven from the circulation of one or another country, but these interferences were not of the persistent and rigid character peculiar to modern monetary legislation. The mistaken belief that the value of the coin might be regulated by the decree of a monarch, or by a legislative enactment, was common to all nations, but whatever the form of the coinage laws recorded in the statute-books, these laws in practice became, in the main, subordinate to the more potent law of individual self-interest.

Under these conditions, and by reason of its greater portability, gold became the metal in which international exchanges were chiefly effected. In the earlier days of commerce, portability was indeed a question of more importance than in our day; a larger sum in gold than in silver could be concealed about the person, and a still larger sum might be carried in a stage-coach without attracting attention. At that day it was hardly safe to confide to any one the location of a *cache* of gold or silver; even monarchs did not always resist the temptation to appropriate it. Charles the First of England stole all the money in the mint, the property of private individuals; he afterwards refunded it, but his son, Charles the Second, was guilty of a similar offence in 1672, and he never returned a shilling of the large sum stolen.

While we have greatly improved the means of transporting the precious metals, insurance against the risks of carriage is still much the larger proportion of the total cost for transport; and as the risks from robbery are greater when gold is carried than when silver is carried, it becomes an open question whether silver is not in many cases the better metal with which to effect distant exchanges. In 1895 some bars of silver, in transit from a railway station in London, were stolen from a dray and recovered by the police only after weeks of search, but the circumstances of the capture showed clearly that if the amount stolen had been in the less bulky gold, the robbers might easily have escaped with their booty.

The currency of England had changed from silver

to gold some years before the passage of the Act of 1816, which decreed gold alone to be the standard; but this change was the result of misdirected legislation, and neither necessary nor a matter of preference on the part of the people. That England's rapid growth in trade and commerce would ultimately have led her people voluntarily to adopt gold as their money may be admitted; but that it did not so occur is a fact to be noted. Through the greater part of the eighteenth century the mint ratio had undervalued silver, and the heavier coins of this metal were consequently melted or exported, thus impairing the uniformity and stability of the silver currency. As early as 1717 the distress occasioned by deterioration and by the want of a sufficient supply of silver money led Parliament to institute an inquiry into the cause of the evil. Sir Isaac Newton was then Master of the Mint, and in his report to the Lords of the Treasury he stated that silver bullion was usually worth from twopence to threepence per ounce more than silver coin, and that at this rate the guinea, which was then current at twenty-one shillings and sixpence, was worth only twenty shillings and eightpence. He also stated that though these figures indicated the usual difference, the price of silver was much higher when there were any ships in port loading for India;—which showed that there was a higher market for silver outside of England. As usual, the action of the government to overcome the evil was on this occasion in the nature of fiat; a royal proclamation was issued prohibiting all persons from uttering or receiving the pieces of gold coin called guineas at any higher rate of value than twenty-one shillings. This still left a margin of profit on the export of the full-weight pieces of silver coin.

English merchants engaged in foreign trade had hitherto computed their bills of exchange in the silver currency of the kingdom, but about this time (1760) they began to make these calculations in gold coin, which, being of the relatively cheaper metal, had not been tampered with. Gold had long been the principal medium of interchange in foreign trade; it now became a measure of value in that trade, but while it may properly be said that gold then became in England the money of international commerce, it was not the money of England. That money was silver, because it was the measure commonly employed by the great body of the people in their domestic transactions.

During this time the volume of gold coin in circulation was steadily increasing, and that of silver relatively declining. By 1760 the shilling pieces in circulation had lost one sixth of their weight, the sixpenny pieces one fourth of their weight, and the larger silver coins had been mostly melted and the metal exported.[1] In 1774 the value of silver, as indicated by the purchases of the Bank of England, began to show a declining tendency; an Act was then passed which limited to twenty-five pounds the amount of silver coin that might be tendered at any one time, but in payments exceeding twenty-five pounds in amount the law allowed an unlimited tender by weight, at the rate of five shillings and twopence per ounce. In 1798 the coinage of silver was suspended; gold may be said to have then, for the first time, become the money of England. The Bank of England had suspended specie payment in the previous year, and did not resume until 1821.

It should be further stated that from the time of Charles the Second (1667), the cost of coining had been borne by the public; any individual might take gold or silver bullion to the mints and have it coined free of seigniorage or any other charge; yet the total amount of silver coined during the eighty-three years from 1717 to 1800 was only £584,764, and this total included all the silver captured in

[1] *Coins of the Realm*, p. 2.

naval warfare during the period named.[1] The testimony is conclusive that, from 1717 to 1771, the ratio fixed by the coinage laws was such as to make it unprofitable for individuals to have silver bullion coined; and that when silver might have been coined without loss, or with profit, the use of silver money was in the first place restricted by the Act of 1774 and then suspended by the Act of 1798, which closed the mints against the coinage of silver for individuals.

[1] *Coins of the Realm*, p. 96.

CHAPTER VII.

HYBRID METALLISM.

ALL the nations of Europe which were not on a gold basis in 1871 have since that date demonetized silver by closing their mints against the coinage of that metal for individual account; but we must not infer from this fact that all of these nations have adopted the English system of gold monometallism. What has really taken place in most of them is the evolvement of a new system of metallic money, distinctly different from the two systems previously existing. Prior to 1871, bimetallism and gold or silver monometallism were the only monetary systems that had been definitely formulated, and every commercial nation had adopted one or the other; but under neither of these systems was the attempt ever made to retain both metals in the circulation by redeeming the coin of one metal in that of the other. In gold monometallic nations silver was admitted into current use only for the purpose of making change, and only a limited amount might be tendered. In England this limit is two pounds. In silver monometallic nations, though silver alone constituted the standard of value, gold was not excluded from use; it therefore circulated at its bullion value in accordance with commercial needs. Holland may be cited as furnishing an example of silver monometallism between the years 1847 and 1875.

Bimetallism assumed to fix a legal ratio at which both metals should be current money; but, as we have seen, under this system coin having a bullion value higher than the adopted ratio was always driven from the circulation, thus leaving one metal as the sole monetary standard; if the other entered into monetary service at all, it did so at its bullion value. This was the experience of the United States and of every other nation which adopted the system of bimetallism prior to 1871.

It will thus be seen that under the earlier monetary laws, when either of the precious metals came into service as the money of a people or as a medium of exchange merely, it always passed at its intrinsic value, and that that value was regulated through domestic and international exchanges by the bullion market of the world. As only one metal can serve as the measure of value for a people at any given time, silver naturally preceded gold in such service, because the lower value of silver better fitted it for the innumerable small transactions of the people as a whole—transactions which still form the bulk of the world's trade.

Now, the new metallism does not reduce silver to the minor service of change-money merely, as was done by the adoption of the gold standard in England, nor does it permit the use of silver at its market value, as was the case in France prior to 1871, when that country was practically on a gold basis. The new metallism is an attempt to combine both metals in one monetary standard by making silver as well as gold an unlimited legal tender at a fixed ratio, and by redeeming the silver coin in gold at that ratio. This system, which for convenience we have named "Hybrid Metallism," is the system now practised by most of the nations which have professedly adopted gold monometallism. To illustrate its workings, we shall again cite Holland, which adopted it in 1875.

Silver alone had been the money of that country previous to 1873, in which year the mints were closed against individual coinage. During the intervening two years there was a contest in the Dutch Parliament as to the adoption of the gold standard, the common people preferring to retain silver money. Trade had been and at the beginning of this term was still very prosperous, but, with closed mints and the metallic circulation thereby limited to a fixed amount, this prosperity could not last. During these two years the market value of silver bullion continually declined, while a demand for more coin than was obtainable increased the purchasing power of the silver florin so that a British sovereign was exchangeable in Holland for less and less silver money. This naturally disturbed foreign exchanges and produced a drain of gold; public confidence was shaken, and a financial crash was only averted by the passage in the Dutch Parliament of the Act adopting the gold standard. Gold might then be coined for individual account, but the government reserved to itself the right to coin silver.

The florin was retained as the monetary unit; a gold coin was issued at the ratio of $15\frac{5}{8}$ of silver to 1 of gold, and the silver florin was decreed to be current money and a full legal tender at that ratio. Silver was thus deprived of its monetary function as a measure of value; it was therefore no longer money in the same sense as it had been between

1847 and 1873. Nor was gold permitted to pass from hand to hand among the people, as it must to constitute the money of a people, and as it does in England to-day. The Bank of the Netherlands was to hold the gold coin, and the people were to carry the silver coin at the factitious value adopted; silver coin was accordingly made an unlimited legal tender.

If we except Germany and the Scandinavian Union, there is no nation in the world to-day that maintains the gold standard in the same sense that England maintains it. All the other nations that since 1871 have joined the movement for a gold standard are now either under a constant strain to maintain their silver coinage in circulation at a gold valuation, or they are floundering upon a paper basis. Economists have long exposed the error and the injustice of giving to paper money the quality of legal tender; upon what principle, then, can we justify the issuance of silver coin which must be accepted at twice its actual value? Is not such coin also *fiat* money? Holland has even imposed this new system of hybrid metallism upon her colonies, where gold coin is never seen passing from hand to hand; even in Amsterdam it can be obtained from the Bank of the Netherlands only if wanted for export. It is this system which prevails in all of the

European nations formerly bimetallic which are not now on a non-convertible paper basis.

Hybrid metallism requires that the State shall hold the gold reserve and assume the responsibility of maintaining at a parity with gold the silver coin in circulation. In Europe this is usually done through the agency of a bank, but this does not alter the fact that it is the action of the State, for without State support and an arbitrary exercise of State power metallic money cannot be maintained in circulation at a value which it does not possess intrinsically. The absolute need of a given volume of metallic money is taken advantage of by the State to keep the circulation filled with silver, and no more gold is permitted to leave the banks than will suffice to redeem any superabundance of silver which may result from the fluctuations of trade. By this means the public is made to carry the silver money, and the gold money is monopolized by the government and the banks. The interests of commerce are considered, but the interests of the working masses are ignored. It is understood that commerce does not admit of the use of metallic money on any other basis than its market value, but it seems not to be understood that the same individual self-interest which governs in commerce also governs labor. The working people and small traders can no more tolerate fiat silver money than can the merchant and the banker.

The working people are supposed not to care what money is paid to them so long as they can "pass it off on their neighbors," but such is not the teaching of monetary history. They may not understand the complexities of exchange or of banking, and they may even believe that the State alone is competent to regulate the value of money, but in their personal dealings they are governed, as are the merchant and the banker, by self-interest. However mistaken or delusive the theories commonly held as to the source from which the coinage derives its purchasing power, the people as a body have always resisted attempts to give it a factitious value; they have instinctively insisted that the nominal and the intrinsic value of their metallic money shall be the same. The debasing of the coinage has often contributed to arouse a feeling of discontent that has culminated in a popular uprising.[1]

We have already stated that the precious metals when not in service as money are floating capital; we may now add that, as such, they are more efficiently

---

[1] J. E. T. Rogers, *The Economic Interpretation of History*, chap. xii.

productive than all other forms of floating capital, and this because they are the money metals. Deprive them of their monetary function as a measure of value, and their power to keep labor and fixed capital productively employed will be reduced to the level of that of nickel, copper, lead, or iron. As money metals they may be everywhere readily exchanged for other commodities, but as metals merely their owner would have to find some one in special need of them before he could effect an exchange. Hence even while the precious metals are still in the form of bullion, and not in service as money, they exert a potential influence on industry over and above their efficiency as capital, and this influence is derived solely from their universal use as money.

The money metal held as capital forms a reserve force to the money metal in actual service as money, and as a reserve force, it inspires that confidence which is essential to industrial prosperity. Though the volume of currency cannot exceed at any given time the limit fixed by the number and value of exchanges, a sufficiency to fill every want of trade at all times is an imperative need, and no nation is secure against financial disaster which has not constantly at command an ample money-metal reserve.

The closing of the mints against the coinage of

silver for individual account, even in one country, diminishes in some degree the applicability of this metal to effect exchanges in the world at large, while in a much greater degree it lowers the productive power of those who are directly debarred from the exercise of their right to have their bullion coined. The closing of the mints of Bombay and Calcutta in 1893 has already had an unfavorable effect upon the trade and industry of British India. Silver is the appropriate money metal for India, because it is relatively less valuable than gold. A day's wages there can be paid with a piece of gold one half or even one quarter the size of an American gold dollar, and a coin so small in proportion to its value cannot be made to circulate in any country. In the United States even the gold dollar could not be kept in circulation, and its coinage had to be discontinued. Metallic money must not only have intrinsic value equal to its nominal value, but it must be of suitable size for handling. These essential principles were entirely ignored by the British government in closing the mints of India against the coinage of silver for individual account.

This government in its action had considered only the interests of commerce; the resulting effects upon the industry of the people as a body were not considered. While the ultimate aim of the government was to give a fixed gold valuation to the rupee circulation, its chief concern was the immediate regulation of the exchangeable value of the rupee with London. The expectation appears to have been that, with closed mints, the value of the rupee might be slowly advanced simply by requiring payment in gold, at a rate fixed upon from time to time for rupees issued from the Treasury. The exchangeable value of the rupee was then one shilling and twopence halfpenny, and the rate fixed upon for the first advance was one shilling and fourpence. The immediate effect of this action was to reduce the exchangeable value of the rupee to one shilling and one penny halfpenny, and to seriously disturb the trade of India with other countries; for several months trade with China almost ceased, and the demoralizing effect upon the entire foreign trade was shown in the official statement of the following year by diminished exports and greatly increased imports. These abortive attempts to give to the rupee an artificial fixed value still continue.

But it was only at the commercial centres that demonetization had any immediate effect upon India; the industrial masses away from these centres had little conception of the great wrong that had been inflicted upon them. The rupee in their estimation had a fixed value, and they had never known a time when silver in any form did not have an exchangeable value equal to the rupee. Their small savings had consequently been invested in silver as the most available property to hold in providing against future contingencies, and famine is one of those contingencies, for in India, as every native knows, famine is of periodical occurrence. Though small when taken singly, these hoardings of silver constitute in the aggregate a vast sum; and the fact that any individual could have his silver coined gave to the whole hoarded mass an availability for conversion into other commodities which it could not otherwise have possessed; an availability which in itself stimulated trade and industry. Closed mints will sooner or later divest the silver of British India of this potential quality. Deprive gold of its monetary function as a common measure of value, and it will sink in productive power to the level of the baser metals as readily as silver will.

While demonetization of silver was steadily progressing in Europe, the price of silver bullion in open market was as steadily declining, dropping fully one third from 1871 to 1892; that demonetization and not over-production was the cause of this decline is evident from the further fall in price which immediately followed the closing of the mints of India in 1893. But notwithstanding the great disparity thus created in the relative value of the two metals in open market, the rupee continued to pass in interior India at a value equal to two shillings sterling. The rupee had lost its exchangeable value in foreign trade, in the exact ratio of the market value of the two metals, but it had not lost its purchasing power at home. To the natives of India the rupee was a fixed measure; their ignorance of monetary principles left them without any guide but their personal experience, and that experience justified their faith in the unchangeable value of the rupee. From 1835, when the government had adopted the Madras rupee as the legal monetary unit for British India, down to 1871, its current and its exchangeable value had been the same.

We are not informed as to the current value or purchasing power of the rupee in the different provinces of British India at the present time, nor is it important to the discussion of the principles under consideration that we should be. We can readily perceive that when the natives of India fully realize that their hoarded silver is no longer convertible into coin, this silver will not only lose its former stimulating influence upon industry, but will eventually sink in value to the level of the bullion market, which is its only available outlet. We may also understand the depressing and discouraging effect that this unexpected change must have upon the toiling masses of India, for it is this class that has hoarded silver. The rich and opulent have held their larger hoardings in gold, because of its smaller bulk in proportion to value; the burden of the great loss caused by the depreciation of silver will therefore fall upon the poor ryot. These changes will necessarily proceed slowly among a people so low in the scale of intelligence, and whose numbers are close upon three hundred millions.

The people of India are instinctively hoarders of the money metals, as indeed are all peoples in the primary industrial stage of civilization. Therefore the government's present monetary policy will divert this hoarding propensity from silver to gold; but as that portion of the circulation which the ryot will be permitted to handle must necessarily be of silver, he will practically be debarred from acquiring gold. In a word, he will not be able to gratify his hoarding propensity, for we may be sure that he will not hoard rupees intrinsically worth only half their nominal value. He is doubtless very stupid, but he will eventually discover the fraudulent character of the rupee, and instinctively he will protect himself; he may be slow in getting there, but he will surely arrive in course of time. Emerson has said that not even a tree is so stupid but that if the earth is taken from its roots it will find it out; and to deprive the ryot of the privilege of hoarding the money metal is to sap the industrial growth of India at its root. Such hoardings constitute the final reserve upon which the State itself may have to fall back in time of extreme need.

There is a vague belief floating in many minds that, because gold is the more valuable metal, it is therefore the better money metal; but the difference in value of the two metals has no significance except as it adapts one or the other to a specific use. On the other hand, stability in value is the most important quality of a money metal. Now the adoption of gold alone as the monetary standard for the world at large would impair the stability of that metal, because it would practically reduce the volume of money metal by one half, and because stability is better maintained by two interchangeable metals than by a single metal. This proposition will be obvious to any one who gives it the least thought. That magnitude of volume conduces to maintain stability in the value of a commodity is as certain as that the ocean, by reason of its great volume, is practically held at a fixed level, while inland seas fluctuate in their level in proportion to their size. And that interchangeable commodities act upon each other to check any sudden rise or fall in their price is a matter of common observation on every commercial exchange. With but one money metal there can, of course, be no interchangeability, and to reduce silver to token money, by constituting gold the only standard of value, is to demonetize silver as effectually as if it had all been manufactured into spoons.

The question is often asked, Why should silver continue to decline in price with its production practically at the maximum, and with such a large production of gold? Since 1892 the gold output has been steadily increasing. It is estimated that by the end of this century, the annual production of the Transvaal alone will be equal to the annual production of the entire globe at the time when that field was opened. Add to this the discovery made last year (1896) in British Alaska, which now gives promise of as large a yield as that of California.

Every market in Europe is now closed against silver, except where it is required for use in the arts, and for this use the supply of demonetized silver at every point is more than sufficient to meet the demand. Oriental markets may continue to take silver, but these, too, must close in the course of time if the demonetizing movement continues. Under such conditions it is useless to attempt any estimate of the actual value of silver or of gold; cost of production can have no effect to regulate their values while such powerful agencies are obstructively influencing the natural market and creating an artificial one for both metals. Not until the stock of silver that has been rejected from monetary service is absorbed in the arts can we have any knowledge of the true relative value of these metals.

As demonetization is the cause, remonetization is the remedy; nothing else can prevent silver from sinking greatly below the average cost of production. This is not a pleasant prospect for the silver-miner, but the outlook does not admit of any other forecast. Silver-mining will certainly be stricken from the list of regular industries if some action be not taken soon by one or more of the leading nations that shall arrest the present false and destructive monetary movement. Very rich mines will doubtless continue to produce silver, and as a by-product it will be produced; but the average mines which have hitherto yielded the bulk of the silver must shut down. In such a crisis, the market would soon find relief in the case of a perishable commodity, but it is not so with silver, which must remain in stock, depressing prices and arresting production until new uses are found for it. And it must be remembered that there are vast hoards of silver in Oriental countries which must ultimately come upon the market if the demonetizing movement be extended into the far East.

Gold is now absorbed by the demonetizing nations faster than it can be produced, and every additional convert to the movement will intensify the scramble for it, as each nation must begin its work by hoarding gold, thus lessening the volume for actual circulation, and increasing the difference in the price of gold and of silver. Russia has already absorbed over $600,000,000 of gold, and Japan is said to have recently bought $5,000,000. Neither of these nations can, in a true sense, establish the gold standard, for silver is the appropriate money metal for both.

As under the rulings of hybrid metallism there is a profit upon every piece of silver that is put into circulation, the question naturally arises—Is it solicitude for the welfare of the people, or is it the allurement of this profit, that has led so many governments within so short a time to adopt the gold standard? This profit, whatever it may be, and it is now over one hundred per cent., is to that extent capital abstracted from the pockets of the people. The capital so taken cannot rightly be called a tax, it is rather a confiscation; because with open mints metallic money cannot circulate in any community at a value below its market value; whereas under the compulsion of closed mints, the people have no choice but to take the hybrid money or resort to barter. Again, this capital is taken so covertly that a proper accounting to the people is seldom made or expected. Here is a temptation to corrupt and wasteful expenditure of the people's resources which very few governments can resist. In 1894 the government of Hayti adopted hybrid metallism, although the people already had a standard admirably suited to their needs—the Mexican silver dollar; yet a company of capitalists, who held control of the public revenue as security for a loan of $20,000,000 made to the government some years previously, had influence enough to effect the change. It would be interesting to know how many governments have acted under similar influences; it may safely be asserted, however, that capitalistic greed is really the force that is impelling the destructive movement.

The objections to hybrid metallism may briefly be summarized as follows:—It has a corrupting influence on government; it sustains the idea that value can be created by legislative enactment, thus teaching the people to look to the State and not to themselves for support; it reduces the productive power of silver as capital to the level of the baser metals; it creates a monopoly in gold by withholding it from the working class; it makes silver coin unfit to be hoarded by this class; it impairs the stability of the standard metal,—gold; it restricts the elasticity of the currency; by undermining the sense of security it retards the growth of credit; it encourages counterfeiting; it weakens the incentive to honest labor. Its general effect is to diminish the productive power of the people, to obstruct and prevent an equitable distribution of the wealth produced, and to lower the standard of morals.

CHAPTER VIII.

CREDIT AS A MONETARY FACTOR, ILLUSTRATED IN THE WORKING OF THE ENGLISH MONETARY SYSTEM.

WHILE it has long been known that the function of credit as a factor in promoting productivity is to economize capital and to facilitate exchanges, its importance is even now but imperfectly understood, and we have but a vague perception of its possible future development. Certain it is that when credit is good, production is increased, and when it is bad there is general depression; the productive forces are checked, and a reduction in the consumption of commodities becomes compulsory.

"Over-production" is the explanation commonly given of these conditions, but over-production is an effect, not a cause. The cause is a contraction of credit, with a consequent derangement of the mechanism which effects the interchange of commodities. A mill-owner finds himself overstocked with finished goods; he therefore shuts down his mill and dismisses his workmen. His goods are floating capital, but they have become for the time fixed capital, because of obstructed avenues of exchange. Other industries are similarly affected, and the stoppage of one necessitates the stoppage of another, for they are in many ways dependent one upon the other, and the finished product of one is often the raw material of another.

On the one side there is idle capital and on the other idle labor, but the two cannot be brought into co-operative activity until sales of goods are effected. Meantime a great many working people are in want of the goods that are stacked up in warehouses, but are without the means to buy because of their enforced idleness. The working people, be it remembered, are the consumers of the bulk of the commodities produced. Commodities may be produced in disproportionate variety, leaving some that are not wanted under any circumstances, but overproduction in the aggregate there cannot be so long as people in need of the commodities are able and willing to work to obtain them. Disproportionate production is, moreover, a local and transient evil which very speedily cures itself, because no one will continue to produce a commodity which cannot be sold; but the condition which has been named "overproduction" may spread over a whole country. This condition does not imply a want of floating capital, for that capital is represented by the goods in store, which, if sold, would set the industries in motion. An insufficiency of floating capital limits the productive powers of a people, but it does not prevent the capital in hand from being utilized to its fullest extent.

A sudden contraction of credit may arise from a variety of causes, as, for example, from a threatened war, or from the failure of a great banking house; from anything, indeed, which shakes public confidence and produces general distrust. But that which is seen to be the immediate occasion of a contraction of credit is seldom the primary cause of such contraction. If we trace these abnormal conditions to their source, we will find it to be, in most instances, the interference of the State with individual freedom to make exchanges.

We have seen that credit in the form of paper money economizes the money metal and imparts the necessary elasticity to the currency. We have also seen that floating capital seeking employment has a tendency to drift to those places where it will be most secure. Profit-making is the end sought by the owner of the capital, but large profit will not attract him unless he feels that his principal is not endangered. Now production is impossible without some amount of floating capital, and if this capital is insufficient there will be idle hands. Without money of some kind, good, bad, or indifferent, trade would cease, and the industrial organism would disintegrate.

A sudden withdrawal of floating capital from the established industries will create a panic, and a sudden contraction of the currency below the needs will also create a panic, but of so different a nature that the first may appropriately be termed a *capital panic*, and the second a *currency panic*. The distinctive difference is that in a capital panic there will be little clogging of the channels of interchange if the currency is sufficiently elastic to meet the exigency. Great quantities of goods will be thrown upon the market at a reduced price, but when these forced sales have ceased and the market has had time to fully absorb the goods, trade will assume normal conditions, and the industries which have not entirely collapsed, but have merely lost a portion of their capital, will move along on a lower plane of productiveness. On the other hand, a currency panic practically arrests exchanges; it affects the entire community, and, while it lasts, is more acutely destructive than a capital panic. A little reflection will show the reason of these differences.

Money, being the medium of exchange and measure of value for a whole community, is in a certain sense the common property of the community, to be used by the members to make exchanges and for this special purpose only. The transfers made in trade between individuals are of capital; they may be of capital for services or of services for capital, but in every case the object of the exchange is capital in some form, and money is simply the instrument employed to measure the value of the capital or of the service, and to effect the exchange. Now, capital is not for the common use, as is money; each individual retains in his possession a certain amount for his own use. For example, in order to build and keep a mill running a certain amount of capital, fixed and floating, is absolutely necessary; this capital must remain in the possession of the owner or of the one who runs the business. The floating capital he may own or he may borrow; but whether owned or borrowed, he must always have it under his control in order to keep his industry in full operation. It is not so with money; the circulation is supposed to be, and should be, sufficient to supply the legitimate needs of every member of the community; no business man thinks of holding more than enough for his immediate wants. Having the floating capital, he feels the same easy confidence that he can procure money when he wants it that the householder has that he can draw water from the city pipes as he needs it.

A capital panic acts directly upon the organized industries that employ much capital and many hands, and it inflicts its severest blows upon the younger and more adventurous undertakings. A currency panic spares no one. A panic of either kind is immediately felt by the banks, inflicting loss upon them. An eminent New York banker has said that no serious financial disturbance occurs which does not cause loss to the banks of that city collectively of from ten to fifteen per cent. of their capital and surplus. In a currency panic, perfectly solvent banks may have to close their doors for want of currency, and factories with ample capital may have to shut down for the same reason. As, however, the immediate cause of both is a contraction of credit, a panic of the one kind is apt to precipitate the other. The panic of May, 1893, in the United States, was distinctly a capital panic, and the panic of August of the same year was as distinctly a currency panic.

The banks are the first to feel a contraction in the volume of currency or a withdrawal of capital from the established industries, because they are the centres of interchange wherever they are located, and banking itself is essentially a growth of credit. The banker's profits are derived mainly from the handling of other people's capital, but this capital cannot be obtained without credit, and its amount will be in proportion to the measure of public confidence which a bank inspires. The deposits of the banks are floating capital, and it is from these deposits that the heads of industries draw a large part of the floating capital employed by them. These deposits are the property of the people at large, and mainly belong to the thrifty working class. In the industrial organism, the working people are naturally the gatherers of floating capital, while the heads of industries are its utilizers. The bankers administer this capital for the people, and it is the duty as well as the interest of the banker to preserve as far as possible a proper proportion between this floating capital, the amount of fixed capital invested, and the number of working people employed. Trading and manufacturing necessitate venture, but banking must be more conservative, and as it is the banker who holds the largest control over the floating capital of a country, it naturally becomes his function, and not that of the State, to supervise the employment of credit and to keep it within legitimate bounds.

In a panic, deposits are rapidly withdrawn from banks, and the banks in their turn as rapidly call in their loans; this capital is then either hoarded by the individual owners, or it is sent to the financial centres for safe keeping. The result is a glut of floating capital at these centres and an insufficient supply in the industrial districts. An exceptionally low rate of interest in London or New York indicates a disturbed equilibrium of capital, and not, as is commonly supposed, a superabundance of it, except at those points. There cannot be a superabundance of capital in the world at large. When money is lent it is capital that is borrowed, and the rate of interest paid on the money is governed by the earning power of the capital; there are, however, exceptions to this rule, due to abnormal economic conditions. An inelastic currency will affect the rate of interest spasmodically, forcing it up or down, but the action of capital upon interest is constant, and is the true regulator, giving a steady rate of interest in each community in proportion to the earning power of the capital employed in the community. A stable rate of interest is essential to trade and industry, a fluctuating rate deters enterprise; hence a steady rate is more important than a low rate of interest.

As the monetary system of England has many influential advocates in the United States who would favor its adoption by this country, it may be well to note its distinguishing features as compared with our own system and with a natural system of money. We shall see that even in England, where the gold standard is a reality and not the hollow sham it is in many other countries, financial panics are of periodical occurrence, as a result of the legislative restrictions imposed upon the use of credit. Notwithstanding that gold coin enters freely into the circulation and is the current money of the people even during a panic, yet since the passage of the famous Banking Act of 1844, designed to regulate the currency automatically and to prevent panics, the Government has three times had to come to the relief of the Bank of England. This Bank suspended gold payment in 1847, in 1857, and again in 1866, and it would have suspended on the failure of the banking house of Baring Brothers in 1890 had not other banks and bankers joined it in assuming the liabilities of that house.

In considering England's monetary system, it is especially with her banking system that we have to deal in connection with our present subject—credit. Her banking system centres in the Bank of England, and is essentially monopolistic in structure. In 1694 certain exclusive rights and privileges were granted to a number of private capitalists in return for a loan of £1,200,000 to the State, and these gentlemen were constituted the Bank of England. From the founding of this Bank to the beginning of the present century, the banking legislation of England would seem to have had no other aim or purpose than to abstract capital from the people to meet the pressing needs of the Government. Every renewal of or change in the Bank's charter was a commercial bargain, the Government obtaining an additional loan and the Bank receiving in return some special privilege. An entire absence of any clear perception of monetary principles marked all these bargainings; they rarely rose in dignity above the level of an ordinary trade transaction between individuals, and as it was through the currency that the desired capital was to be obtained, Government and Bank conspired to weaken competition in this field, and to secure for the Bank of England a monopoly of note issue. As early as 1708, on the first renewal of the Bank's charter, an Act was passed forbidding all banking companies of more than six partners to utter notes payable in less than six months from the date of issue. And as in all banking companies, whether private or chartered, the partners were individually liable for all the debts of their respective companies, and as the shareholders of the Bank of England were exempted from such liability, the law had a potent influence in preventing persons of wealth from engaging in the business of banking. This law remained in force until 1826.

Under these centralizing influences the banking system of England attained its first hundred years or more of growth, the trade of the country meantime necessarily adapting itself to the existing conditions. The Bank of England was then, as now, the depository for the Government, and it gradually became the centre of the whole banking system, all other banks and bankers treating their deposits in this one as so much cash in hand. Artificial in construction, the system is like a pyramid inverted, and needs constant governmental propping, not only to preserve the Bank of England, but to prevent a collapse of the entire superstructure, of which credit is an essential and a component part.

Contrast this system with one in which each bank would keep its own reserve, and we shall see that the latter system not only rests upon a more substantial foundation, but its tendency is to promote greater watchfulness on the part of the individual banks and a more careful employment of credit by them, while the tendency of the former is to relieve the banks of their responsibility in these respects, and to encourage irregular banking. Public confidence is essential to the maintenance of any system of banking, and it must be admitted that the confidence of Englishmen in their system is absolute, but this confidence rests not so much upon the large capital of the Bank of England, or upon its good management, as upon the fact that the Government stands ready to protect the Bank when it gets into trouble. Every Englishman knows that "the Government is close behind the Bank, and will help it when wanted," and "most Englishmen would think as soon of winding up the English nation" as of putting the Bank into liquidation.[1]

If during a financial crisis the Bank of England finds itself in trouble, in what way can it be helped

---

[1] Bagehot, *Lombard Street*, p. 40.

with justice to its creditors and all concerned but by supplying the gold necessary to enable it to meet its demand payments? But this is not the course taken by the British Government when it comes to the aid of the Bank; on the contrary, the Government releases the Bank from the obligation to pay in gold, and authorizes it to issue notes to any extent until the pressure for currency shall be relieved and public confidence restored. And as the English Banking Act has made these notes a legal tender for all debts, public and private, except at the counter of the Bank, when the Bank is thus released from paying them in gold, they become fiat money. This practically bars the Bank's creditors from collecting their dues; they must accept the Bank's promises to pay, and await its convenience for their fulfilment. It is consequently at the cost of its creditors that the Bank of England is saved from impending liquidation.

It is, of course, better that the Government should relax its restraint upon the use of credit and permit an unlimited issue of notes, than to take the alternative of closing the Bank, which would involve the country in vastly greater and more extended loss; but does not the fact that the Government must stand by the Bank exhibit the artificial character and inherent weakness of the one-reserve system? A system which makes it necessary as a measure of self-preservation for well-managed solvent banks to assume the liabilities of a bank which may have become insolvent through mismanagement, is certainly not calculated to promote banking integrity or banking efficiency. It was not a voluntary act of the banks and bankers to assume the $100,000,000 liabilities of Baring Brothers in 1890. There would doubtless continue to be individual instances of irregular banking under any system that might be adopted, but a system which inflicts its penalties alike upon the offending and the unoffending is surely to be avoided rather than copied by the United States.

Although our monetary laws are about as incongruous as they can be, our monetary system has no defects so deeply rooted that they need seriously obstruct the introduction of a free system of money. This favorable condition in the United States is due to an inherent and instinctive feeling that has always largely prevailed among the people, influencing them to oppose any monetary legislation that seemed to them to savor of monopoly. Twice in our history this feeling has successfully and beneficially asserted itself; once in 1811 in opposition to the renewal of the charter of the first United States Bank, and again in 1836 when it prevented the renewal of the charter of the second United States Bank; both of these enactments being attempts to fasten upon the country a great centralizing National bank similar to the Bank of England. It cannot be doubted that the popular agitation of to-day may be quieted by the establishment of open mints and free banking, which are essential features of a true system of money, without which any system would be incompatible with our form of government.

A natural outcome of independent banking is the formation of a Clearing-House Association at each trade centre; there are now eighty-four of these organizations in the United States. They are formed primarily by the banks to facilitate exchanges among themselves, but they lead to co-operation on other lines to the advantage of the banks and of the country at large. The fluctuations of trade in any locality are more distinctly seen and felt behind the bank counter than in front of it, while within each clearing-house a still more extended knowledge is obtained of these changes as they occur from day to day. Through these organizations the strength that comes from combination and from knowledge is acquired without any sacrifice of individual freedom, and without involving any bank member in liabilities which are not voluntarily assumed. Banking is inherently individual in its nature, each bank being in itself a local centre of exchanges; it is therefore important that each bank should hold and control its own reserve, but as all banking is vitally dependent upon public confidence, self-interest naturally leads to systematized action among the banks to sustain such confidence. Irregular banking is not tolerated in these voluntary and self-governing clearing-house organizations; each bank is held strictly to its obligations, and each must report its condition to the Association at stated intervals; it will be found that all the regulations of these Associations contribute to promote banking efficiency and to elevate the standard of banking integrity.

The one-reserve system was not a natural growth, nor was it deliberately adopted by the bankers and traders of England; it was, as we have seen, a consequence of the exclusive privileges granted to the Bank of England through a long period before any definite theory of banking had been formulated. When economic principles came to be generally discussed, changes looking to the public welfare were made in the banking laws, the Act of 1844 constituting the basis of the present system. The ideas embodied in this enactment may be traced to what is termed the Bullion Report, made by a Committee of Parliament in 1810. Sir Robert Peel, who had entered Parliament in the previous year, was a member of this committee, and he was Premier when the Act of 1844 was passed. The Bullion Report is a remarkable production; in the elucidation of monetary principles it is greatly in advance of the popular thought of the time. The accepted opinion then was, even in Lombard Street, that there was no necessity for requiring the redemption of bank notes in coin on demand. This theory was supported by the Governor of the Bank of England, by the Deputy-Governor, and by one of the directors, as shown by their testimony given before the committee. The views entertained by these gentlemen, and by Englishmen generally, in reference to paper money, were similar to those advocated fifty years later in the United States by the Greenback party; the Bullion Report exposed the fallacy of these views, and established the principle that paper money must be redeemable in coin on demand.

At the time when the Bullion Report was made, economic teaching had had no influence upon legislation; Adam Smith's *Wealth of Nations* had been generally read by scholars, and other works of the same nature had appeared in England, but the ideas they propounded had made no perceptible impression upon the popular mind, which may be accounted for by the fact that England had been almost continuously engaged in war from 1776 (the year in which the *Wealth of Nations* was published) to 1815. The thirty years succeeding 1815 were years of great industrial depression and general discontent; they were also years of profound study and of popular discussion of the causes which had brought the nation to this unhappy state. English economic literature of that period cannot fail to impress the student with the intellectual ability then displayed in the discovery and exposition of fundamental principles, nor in comparing that period with our own will he fail to perceive the lapse which has taken place in the popular recognition of economic truths. Protection to the individual in his rights of property, and freedom to make exchanges are the basic principles of all economic teaching, and these ideas had during this period of thirty years settled down into the common sense of the nation. As a result of this mental awakening the current of legislation now set towards greater individual freedom, and it is specially to be noted that the legislative changes which followed were mainly the repealing of enactments which had obstructed the channels of interchange. Restrictions which bore directly upon trade were removed or put in the way of removal by the adoption of legislative measures providing for ultimate free trade. But while it was generally conceded that trade must be left absolutely untrammelled, it was not recognized that an equal freedom is essential for money and banking.

The instructions of Parliament to the Bullion Committee were " to inquire into the cause of the high price of gold bullion, and to take into consideration the state of the circulating medium and of the exchanges between Great Britain and foreign parts." The currency of England had been on an inconvertible paper basis since 1797. Napoleon's threatened invasion of England had led the Government to restrict the Bank of England from redeeming its notes in coin, and as these notes were an unlimited legal tender, they became and continued until 1821 to be the common standard of value for the United Kingdom. All other bank notes were redeemable in the notes of the Bank of England. This paper currency consequently fell below its par value, and the gold money became a merchantable commodity which fluctuated in price from day to day to the great embarrassment of merchants engaged in foreign trade. The general belief, however, was not that a depreciation in the value of the paper money had taken place, but that there had been a rise in the value of gold. It was argued that gold had become scarce because of the demand for it on the Continent for military purposes, and because of individual hoarding.

In combating this argument the Bullion Committee exhibited a knowledge of fundamental monetary principles which were familiar to students of political economy, but of which the general public was entirely ignorant. The Committee showed by conclusive testimony that there had been no scarcity of gold to those who were willing to pay the premium, that the value of gold on the Continent and in England had varied but slightly, and that these variations were sufficiently accounted for by the cost of transport from one country to another—a cost that had been increased by an obstructive law and by war risks. The argument of the Committee was in substance that as "a given quantity of gold itself can never be exchanged for a greater or less quantity of gold of the same standard fineness," it follows that, so long as gold may be freely exported and imported, a rise in the value must be general, and cannot be confined to England or to any one country. "A diminution or increase in the general supply of gold will no doubt have a material effect upon the money prices of all other articles," but can have no effect upon the money itself, if that money be of gold. A rise in the value of money will undoubtedly cause a fall in the prices of all commodities, but, "that this is not the present state of things is manifest, the prices of all commodities have risen, and gold appears to have risen in price only in common with them. If this common effect is to be ascribed to one and the same cause, that cause can only be found in the state of the currency."

This, in brief, was the answer of the Committee to the advocates of the erroneous views then generally entertained in reference to the currency. It was, however, many years before the theory of money as presented in the report of the Committee came to be accepted by the public. By the promotion of monetary knowledge this Committee had rendered an important service not only to England, but to the world at large; it had established two basic principles: first, that the only value a current coin can possess above an equal weight of bullion of the same fineness is the small cost of minting; and second, that in no way can paper money be uniformly maintained at its nominal value in the circulation except by its redemption in coin on demand at that value. By thus placing the metallic standard squarely upon its commercial value, the Committee had undermined the fiat theory of money; a theory which, however, still lingers foggily in England, and which dominates the monetary legislation of all other nations.

But while the Bullion Committee executed in the most thorough manner the work for which it had been appointed, it did not extend its researches beyond this special service. It showed that the standard metal must be free from legal restrictions, and it therefore advised that the law which prohibited the export of British gold should be repealed, but it saw nothing wrong in the restrictions which had been imposed upon silver. The Committee was deeply impressed with the importance of a stable currency, and the need of an expanding and contracting volume it also recognized, but it did not realize how imperative this need was, nor had it the remotest perception that a sufficiently elastic currency could be secured only through a free use of credit. In a general way the importance of credit was emphasized, yet it was held to be the duty of the Government to confine the use of it, so far as the currency was concerned, within artificially fixed limits. The Committee recognized that there was a distinction between money and capital, but the precise service that each performed it did not clearly perceive.

The principles of money, as presented in the report of the Bullion Committee, had been generally accepted before the Act of 1844 was passed, and this Act, with the supplementary Act of 1845, is the practical embodiment of those principles. In securing the passage of these Acts, Sir Robert Peel had evidently determined to keep the control of the currency in the hands of the Government. The right to issue notes was denied to all banks coming into existence in any part of the United Kingdom after the passage of these Acts. Such banks in England and Wales as already had notes in circulation were limited in their issue to the amount then out, and if any one of them retired from business, or surrendered its circulation, the right to issue two thirds of the amount of such circulation reverted to the Bank of England. The same restriction was laid upon banks of issue in Scotland and Ireland, but with the privilege of such additional issue as was fully covered by coin or bullion.

Note issue was assumed to be a separate and distinct business from banking; the Bank of England was therefore divided into an Issue and a Banking Department. The latter department the Bank Governors are free to manage in their own way; but the Issue Department, over which they are permitted to preside, though they do not control it, is practically a Government Bureau. The terms upon which notes may be issued and redeemed are specially fixed by law, and the Bank Governors have no more discretion in the matter than have our Treasury officials over the notes which they issue and redeem. Indeed, Bank of England notes are in equity as truly Government paper money as are United States gold certificates, silver certificates, greenbacks, and Treasury notes, for, though the Bank alone is legally bound to redeem its notes, the Government has taken to itself their exclusive control, it has endowed them with the property of legal tender, and it shares with the Bank the profit arising from their circulation.

The total issue of Bank of England notes is about £60,000,000, of which £16,800,000 is issued against Government and other securities, all notes above this sum being fully covered by bullion, one fifth of which may be in silver. The circulation of Great

Britain and Ireland can at no time contain, therefore, more credit notes than was fixed by the limit of 1844-45. By *credit notes* is meant notes which the issuing banks are legally bound to redeem in coin on demand, but against which they are not legally bound to hold any specified amount of securities or bullion, that being left to the discretion and business judgment of the bankers. This form of paper money has the largest measure of elasticity, and a sufficiently elastic currency to meet the requirements of modern trade can only be obtained by the use of such money at all local centres of exchange. Whether or not bank notes against which securities must be held are more elastic than metallic money depends upon the terms of their issue, but notes against which coin must be held to their full nominal value are practically metallic money.

Sir Robert Peel's theory of trade was that financial panics, which are of periodical occurrence in every commercial country, are caused by overtrading, and as this theory is even now commonly accepted, it will be necessary to consider it in connection with the analysis just given of the Bullion Committee's theory of money, in order clearly to perceive the idea which governed the framing of the banking law, and also to point out some defects of that law. This theory assumes, first, that if banks are not restricted to a fixed limit of note issue, they will so far over-issue as to provoke over-trading, lower the value of the paper circulation, and cause a rise in the price of commodities; second, that these high prices will increase imports and decrease exports, thus creating an indebtedness to foreign countries which must be paid in gold, the drain of which from the country will produce collapse.

A currency that is dissevered from its metallic base will inevitably fluctuate in value and will thereby stimulate speculative dealing, but such dealing is not trading, and *over-trading* there cannot be. Trading is but the exchange of one commodity for another; if there were no commodities there could be no trading. To produce commodities there must be floating capital, and to facilitate exchanges in these commodities there must be money. Production is, in fact, a reproduction of floating capital with increase, the increase being the product of skill, labor, and floating capital combined. To produce at all the workmen must have food, clothing, tools, etc., and these things are all commodities, in other words, floating capital. Society being constituted upon a basis of co-operation and mutual dependence, the producer consumes only a small part of his product, and exchanges his surplus with producers of other articles in order to supply his various wants; the trader effects these exchanges, thus developing a separate occupation, and one upon which production is dependent. If commodities could not be exchanged, co-operative production would cease; each family would have only such quantity and variety of goods as it produced within itself, which would throw civilization back to the conditions of barbarism. Hence it follows that the more readily commodities can be exchanged, the greater will be their production and the more there will be of them to divide for consumption and for reproduction. A free exchange of commodities between two individuals can never be an injury to others; but, as trading promotes productiveness, its restriction injuriously affects the whole community. To restrict or interfere with trading is therefore a perversion of the function of government.

Speculative dealing in commodities is a kind of gambling that will produce all the evils attributed to " over-trading "; we must therefore conclude that it is to such dealings that this term is applied. These are conducted with no other object than the gain that may be acquired from the daily fluctuations in market price. A thousand bushels of wheat turned over speculatively a thousand times does not add one grain of wheat to the total product, yet a vast amount of capital may be absorbed in these dealings—capital which, if employed in production, will result not only in benefit to the producer, but to the entire community. A government cannot prohibit such dealings, however, without interfering with legitimate trade and producing consequences more disastrous to the general welfare than the speculation itself. Bona-fide buyers of the goods who hold them for future markets, even though they are prompted solely by the incentive of profit, are performing an important service to the community at large; they are the carriers of the reserve stock which is the necessary safeguard against scarcity or famine, and which besides exerts a salutary influence upon the market in preserving uniformity and stability in price.

Under natural conditions, the volume of trade is limited by the volume of floating capital, and the volume of currency is limited by the volume of trade. But under the artificial conditions of an unstable currency, prices are abnormally stimulated and speculation is incited; every speculative transaction withholds or abstracts floating capital from legitimate trade or industry and further stimulates prices. As prices are thus forced up, more and more capital is required to carry the stock, and more and more money is required to effect exchanges. But as the volume of floating capital in a country is at any given time limited to a given amount, these rapid advances in price are nothing more than an expansion of credit. Legitimate trading, through the stimulus it gives to industry, is continuously re-enforced with floating capital from that source, but not so with speculative dealing; it feeds upon the capital in existence, and by its abstractions from industry arrests production. Meantime the high prices make it profitable to import goods and unprofitable to export them, thus disturbing the balance of trade and creating an indebtedness to foreign countries which must be paid in the money metal.

The great object of Sir Robert Peel in procuring the passage of the Banking Act, was to create a currency that would, in the words of the Bullion Report, "secure substantial justice and faith of moneyed contracts and obligations between man and man"; a noble object, surely, and one worthy of the statesman whose whole political career had been marked by a high sense of the obligations of his public trust. But as the essential principles governing trade and banking were not fully understood, some were considered and others were unheeded in framing the Banking Act, with the result that it failed to accomplish the purpose for which it was intended. It was thought that by the limitation of the use of credit in the currency, the volume of trade would be kept within its legitimate channels, and that a recurrence of financial panics would thus be averted; yet the law had been hardly three years in operation when a panic supervened, which obliged the Government to come to the aid of the Bank of England. The cause of this panic (1847) and the working of the banking law in reference to it, must now be considered.

Since the beginning of the century improvements in tramway carriage for coal had been steadily progressing, and by 1830 George Stephenson had added his improved locomotive, and had built the railway for general traffic and travel from Liverpool to Manchester, which proved a great success. This at once gave an impetus to railway building; new roads were started in every available locality until the number projected far exceeded the ability of the nation to build them. Railway building is a conversion of floating into fixed capital, and projects of this nature can never be extended beyond a limit fixed by the amount of floating capital existing in the country at the time. In our day railways are an indispensable part of the industrial mechanism, but nothing is gained by building them before they are needed. Though the railway itself produces nothing, it facilitates and cheapens the carriage of goods, and is thus an auxiliary to production. In productive industry the volume of floating capital increases in a geometrical ratio; but as this increase is proportioned to the amount of floating capital employed, and as the railway is dependent for its traffic upon the amount of goods produced, to abstract floating capital from active industry in order to build railways, is to depress and not to assist production. By 1847, the diversion of floating capital from the established industries of England had produced a general collapse; not until shipments of gold arrived from the newly-discovered mines of California can it be said that trade and industry had assumed their normal conditions. Having in addition the larger individual freedom which resulted from the repeal of restrictive laws, England now entered upon a period of great prosperity, more than doubling her foreign trade within seven years.

The banking law of England had not only failed to exert a restraining influence over the wild stock-jobbing in railway property which culminated in

1847, but it had actually contributed to provoke the evil and to intensify the crisis when it came. The Government, having taken to itself the regulation of the currency, had relieved the bankers of their responsibility in this respect, and had thus practically dismissed from service the natural guardians of the public credit. Anything that disturbs the equilibrium of trade increases the risks of trading and incites to speculative dealing. An unstable currency, as we have seen, has that effect; but every restriction to the freedom of interchange has a similar effect, and to deny to the banker his right to issue credit notes, is to restrict and demoralize trade in its beginnings. To deny this right is to sever a bond of mutual dependence and co-operation between the banker and his customers, and thus to weaken the watchful supervision of the banker at the very time when it would be most effective in checking speculative dealing. To compel banker and customer to look to the State and not to themselves for their common medium of exchange, increases its cost to them and obliges them to economize its use and to resort to methods which are less direct—to the use of checks, time notes, and book accounts into which credit may freely enter. It is at the outset of a trade transaction that a legitimate use of credit must be enforced, and as each bank is in itself a centre of exchange, it is at each one of these centres, and not merely at a Government Bureau, that the proper checks must be applied to prevent a misuse of credit. No government is competent to this task, it is the province of the banker.

We shall now briefly recapitulate the distinctive functions of capital, money, and credit, in order to present as convincingly as may be some concluding considerations of the banking law of England. Floating capital gives direct effect to skill, labor, fixed capital, and to all kindred producing forces; money facilitates the exchange and distribution of commodities, and thus stimulates production; credit performs a double service—it not only economizes floating capital and thus preserves a larger amount for production, but by imparting elasticity to the currency and in its various uses by the banker and the trader, it facilitates exchanges.

It must not be overlooked that the final object of all these appliances is production, and it must specially be noted that money and credit are auxiliary forces which support and greatly enhance the productive power of capital. It follows therefore that whenever credit is employed in a way that does not contribute to productiveness, it is misused. It is so misused, as we have seen, when employed in speculative dealing, which not only produces nothing but which lessens production by its abstractions of floating capital from industry. Credit, when legitimately employed, always represents capital; it is always a promise to pay in capital, and if it appears among the transactions of trade without any capital to back it, it is misused. Now let us see whether the English banking law contributes to eliminate the non-productive or fraudulent use of credit from the trade of England.

It may be asked what was the object of dividing the Bank of England into an Issuing and a Banking Department. The Governors of the Bank are in charge of both departments, consequently it is upon their good faith that the Government must depend for the maintenance of the gold reserve, and for the issue and redemption of notes as prescribed by law. Under these circumstances would it not have been as well to allow the Governors to consult their own convenience in the internal arrangements of the Bank as to establish this arbitrary division? The arrangement may possibly facilitate the clerical working of the Bank, but so far as the public is concerned, it has no significance. In adopting this regulation the framers of the banking law were under the impression that it would be a check upon the directors in paying out gold; but in this they simply betrayed their misconception of the relation of the Bank to its customers and of the nature of capital and money. So long as the Bank continues to meet its obligations, the depositors have the same control over the gold in the Issue Department as the bill-holders have.

When a panic occurs the money in circulation is held in the firm grasp of the public, and the draft upon the Bank is of floating capital; it is the deposits that are drawn upon, and the Governors have no option but to pay every valid demand claim upon the Bank or close its doors. When the Bank makes payment in notes, gold may be demanded for them at the Issue Department; the notes are then cancelled. If this gold be exported, it is floating capital and not money that is sent out of the country. This draining process may go on until the Banking Department is emptied of its currency, then it must stop for lack of a medium to effect the transfers. The Bank can then obtain a further supply of currency only by forced sales of its securities; but as such selling would, if persisted in, so far shake public confidence as to drive all credit from trade and reduce prices of commodities far below their normal value, it would soon involve the Bank and the country at large in a general crash. When therefore the Bank has exhausted its currency reserve it has practically reached the end of its tether, and nothing can be done to prevent a collapse but to permit the use of credit notes; this the Government immediately proceeds to do.

In the panic of 1847, the Bank did not find it necessary to use the privilege granted to it of issuing credit notes, and the question suggests itself why, under such urgent conditions, should it have been unnecessary? The explanation is that the crisis had already accomplished its work of destruction so far as capital was concerned; baseless credit and the productive forces of the country had been equally stricken down, but the currency had not been materially affected. At the stage at which it stopped the crisis was therefore a capital panic; the action of the Government at this juncture, in relaxing its grip upon credit, had so far restored public confidence as to save the country from the further infliction of a currency panic. The conversion of floating into fixed capital, however, had been carried to such an extent that there was an insufficiency of floating capital for the industries of the nation, which could move therefore only on a lower plane of productiveness. Not until additional floating capital was produced or brought in from abroad could there be any forward movement in industry. The panic had left a wreckage of trade transactions to be gathered up and adjusted, and credit had to be fully restored before even the existing capital of the kingdom could be fully utilized, which required time to accomplish. It was two years before an industrial revival was distinctly noticeable, and this improvement was then further stimulated by the arrival of gold from the new fields of California.

While the general business of the country was still under the greatest strain, an excess of gold was circulating as money, yet no part of it could be made available as capital, because of the absolute need of a sufficient volume of currency for purposes of exchange. The banking law had unquestionably forced a large amount of gold into general use; but the use of force had robbed the metal of a most necessary element—freedom. In shackling credit, it had also shackled gold. To retain British gold in the kingdom was the object of the Act that prohibited its export, which Act was repealed because the Bullion Committee had shown it to be obstructive and mischievous; yet the framers of the banking law, having no realization of the double service performed by gold as money and as capital, did not perceive that their law would have precisely the same defects. The gold in the currency was now even more effectually barred from export than gold in general had been by the prohibitive Act, for until credit entered into the currency, gold could not come out. Nor did the framers of the banking law perceive that the domestic trader and the banker must be equally free with the foreign trader; that they were co-ordinate and mutually dependent forces working to one common end—namely, to facilitate exchanges and thereby increase the productive power of the nation; that freedom could not be denied to one without affecting the freedom of the others; that the credit note was in domestic trade the counterpart of the bill of exchange in foreign trade; that to maintain stability in the value of the currency it was as essential that gold should be free to pass out or into the circulation as that gold should be freely exported and imported.

The Bullion Committee had shown by the most ample testimony that no person who was willing to pay the premium on gold had ever had any difficulty in obtaining all he wanted. It had also shown that the premium on gold was caused by the failure of the Government to enforce payment of demand notes in that metal, and by the obstructive export law; and that, with these errors corrected, no difference in the value of gold in England and on the Continent could exist beyond the small cost of transport from one country to another. By thus limiting the Government's action to its proper function of enforcing the obligation of contract, and by requiring its non-interference in other respects, this Committee had shown and proved that individual freedom is an essential element of monetary law. The banking law is therefore in conflict with this established principle; it sacrifices to mere bulk and quantity the high qualities of stability and efficiency which gold derives from freedom; it ignores and frustrates the natural law of mutual dependence between bankers and their customers, which secures their united action in maintaining the integrity and efficiency of the currency; it thus incites speculative dealing, and when these dealings culminate in general disaster, the Government has no relief to offer but a temporary modification of the law's arbitrary ruling against credit.

The panic of 1847 ought in itself to have convinced the English people that their banking law had practically failed in its purpose, and we need not doubt that such would have been their decision had it not been for the vague superstition that prevails in regard to money. If a ship when launched could not float erect, but should turn bottom up, there would be no mystery about it; common sense would at once declare that its construction was defective. But it is altogether different when the subject treated is money and banking; the fiat idea bulks so largely to the public eye that practical experience is set aside and common sense is held in abeyance. So it has come to be a common belief that panics are natural and necessary phenomena which expel from the trade of a country evils that cannot otherwise be avoided; that in some unexplained way they clear the commercial atmosphere as a thunderstorm clears the physical atmosphere. Panics are in every sense destructive, and are no more unavoidable than an epidemic of Asiatic cholera is unavoidable; both strike down without distinction the strong and the weak; if we would apply to panics the same intelligent tracing of effect to cause that has enabled the physician to make a cholera epidemic a thing no longer to be dreaded, they too would cease to be a menace.

After each regular sitting of the directors of the Bank of England, the rate of discount is publicly announced, and this custom compensates in some degree for the defective working of a banking system which is eminently artificial and out of accord with natural conditions. We must not infer, however, that these announcements are made with a view to regulate the rate of interest, for that is governed by the earning power of capital, and is therefore beyond the control of the Bank. As the centre of the monetary system of a nation whose commercial dealings extend all over the globe, the Bank occupies a position which gives its directors the widest attainable knowledge of the drift of, and demand for, floating capital. In this respect the Bank's position in the financial world is not unlike that of our Signal Service Bureau in regard to the weather. With its superior advantages for noting the movement of capital, the Bank is able to forecast approaching changes in the rate of interest, and very properly avails itself of this knowledge in the conduct of its business. The movement of floating capital is governed by two considerations—security and earning power; ample security attracts capital, and an abundant supply of capital lowers the rate of interest in proportion to earning power. In other words, the rate of interest, is affected first, by the degree of security, and second by the supply of, and demand for, floating capital; but that which finally fixes the rate paid for borrowed capital is its earning power at the point where it is employed. Under these natural conditions, the rate of interest at any given point will be a steady rate, provided that the currency is stable in value and its volume free to expand and contract with the demands of trade. As, however, the currency of England lacks such elasticity, there is an abnormal degree of fluctuation in the rate of interest, which is a cause of serious disturbance to legitimate trade and industry. The frequency of the changes made in the Bank's rate of discount is a subject of constant complaint, but no blame should attach to the directors on this account, as the fault is entirely in the banking system. As well might a shipmaster who is ready to sail find fault with the Weather Bureau for signalling an impending storm.

A State can always suspend specie payment or evade its obligations, and no State has ever failed to exercise this power at one time or another; but it must be admitted that no nation has maintained the integrity of its money more uniformly than England has. From the twelfth century to the present time, with the single exception of a short period towards the close of Henry the Eighth's reign and at the beginning of Edward the Sixth's, the coinage of England has been kept at such uniform fineness as to have made the word *sterling* a synonym for good quality. Debasement of the coinage, which either reduced the size of the pieces or the amount of precious metal in them, was practiced in Europe to a much greater extent than it ever was in England. Her pound sterling, originally a pound weight of silver, was at different times reduced in weight and value by increasing the number of shillings coined from the pound, which was originally twenty shillings, and finally came to be sixty-six, with the sub-divisions of the shilling correspondingly reduced. But as the purity of the metal was preserved, and as down to the reign of Queen Elizabeth every householder had his money scales and weighed the pieces, the filchings of the monarch fell altogether upon the poorer classes, who received and paid the pieces by tale. Let us not assume, however, that in our more civilized age such dishonesty is obsolete, for the acts of the monarch were but petty pilferings in comparison with the despoiling of the laboring classes perpetrated through hybrid metallism.

The good name that England's silver money had acquired in the past has undoubtedly had its influence in gaining for her the position she now occupies as the financial centre of the globe, but it is chiefly through the protection that she gives to property and through the freedom allowed in effecting exchanges that she has earned this position, and with it a controlling command of the world's floating capital. England is in the very best of credit because everywhere it is understood that she has the disposition as well as the power to protect the rights of every man, native or foreigner, who holds property under her jurisdiction; the sense of security thus inspired is the foundation of her prosperity. To inspire such confidence, the power to protect is as essential as the disposition to do so; in this respect the insular position of England gives her an advantage over the Continental nations, which are more exposed to invasion, but the commercial freedom enjoyed by her people is of her own choice.

In closing this work attention must be called, as it was in beginning it, to the fact that the popular movement against the demonetization of silver is founded upon a real grievance, and that therefore it cannot be put down by quoting high authorities nor by imputing dishonest motives to the advocates of free coinage. The remarkable progress made in our day in scientific discovery, which has led to such beneficent results, has been made not by submissively accepting established authorities, but by questioning them. If the theory of money presented in this work is not utterly at fault, the silver question must be settled by a recognition of the principles advocated and by the formulation of monetary laws in accordance with them, or it will settle itself by the suspension of gold payment and the use of silver money at its bullion value; there is no other way in which it can be settled. A system of money which in any degree hampers the productive powers of a people cannot withstand the natural forces that are impelling improvement in every appliance that contributes to productiveness, and as the natural order of displacement of one metal by another can only proceed when the money of both metals is passing at its bullion value, persistence in the attempt to forestall this natural order must result ultimately in the overthrow of the artificial system.

WORLD'S PRODUCTION OF GOLD AND SILVER.

Table showing the ratio of the production of silver to that of gold during the periods named.

YEARS.	GOLD. Number of ounces produced.	SILVER. Number of ounces produced.	RATIO OF SILVER TO GOLD.
1601–1620	5,478,360	271,924,700	49.64
1621–1640	5,336,900	253,084,800	47.42
1641–1660	5,639,110	235,530,900	41.77
1661–1680	5,954,180	216,691,000	36.39
1681–1700	6,921,895	219,841,700	31.76
1701–1720	8,243,260	228,650,800	27.74
1721–1740	12,268,440	277,261,600	22.60
1741–1760	15,824,230	342,812,235	21.66
1761–1780	13,313,315	419,711,820	31.53
1781–1800	11,438,970	565,235,580	49.41
1801–1820	9,395,195	461,326,780	49.10
1821–1840	11,093,357	339,828,715	30.63
1841–1851	17,605,018	250,903,422	14.25
1851–1870	125,581,276	680,187,904	5.42
1871–1890	102,460,000	1,623,768,000	15.85
1601–1890	356,553,506	6,386,759,956	17.91

The figures for 1601 to 1870 are taken from Dr. Soetbeer's tables; those for 1871 to 1890 from tables compiled by John S. Hanson and published by the Fourth National Bank of the City of New York, in 1896.

FROM DR. SOETBEER'S TABLES.

Showing the relative value of silver to gold, arranged by periods of several years.

YEARS.	Oz. Silver for 1 oz. Gold.	YEARS.	Oz. Silver for 1 oz. Gold.
1661–1680	15.00	1801–1810	15.61
1681–1700	15.00	1811–1820	15.51
1701–1710	15.27	1821–1830	15.80
1711–1720	15.15	1831–1840	15.75
1721–1730	15.09	1841–1850	15.83
1731–1740	15.07	1851–1855	15.41
1741–1750	14.93	1856–1860	15.30
1751–1760	14.56	1861–1865	15.40
1761–1770	14.81	1866–1870	15.55
1771–1780	14.64	1871–1875	15.97
1781–1790	14.76	1876–1880	17.81
1791–1800	15.42	1881–1885	18.63

INDEX.

A

Absorption of gold by demonetizing nations, 124
Act that demonetized silver, the, 77
Act that fixed the ratio, the, 77
Annual product of silver in the United States, 5
Atkinson's, Edward, statement of the annual product of silver in the United States, 5
Average annual product of gold and silver, 82, 83

B

"Bad" and "good" money, 34, 37
Bagehot, Walter, cited, 36, 55
Bank, deposits, 57; auditing, 61
Bank of Dundee, statement of the, 59
Bank of England, suspended specie payment, 106; the centre of the English banking system, 136, 137; founding of the, 136; first renewal of the charter of the, 137; Englishmen's faith in the, 138; notes are fiat money, 139; Issue and Banking departments of the, 150; notes are government money, 150; total issue of notes of the, 150; rate of discount of the, 166-168
Bank of France, the action of, 16, 97; the world's balance-wheel, 101
Banks, parent and individual, contrasted, 62
Banker, duties of a, 133
Banking system of Scotland, 45; in Canada, 47
Bimetallism, 5; radical defect of, 6; in France, 15; working of, 109
Bimetallic league, international, 17
Bland Act, passage of the, 6; effect of the, 6; a dead letter, 75
British Alaska, production of gold in, 122

British Chancellor of the Exchequer on the choice of a monetary standard, 95
Bullion Committee, instructions of Parliament to the, 145; knowledge of monetary principles of the, 146; answer to Parliament of the, 147; work of the, 148, 154
Bullion market, interferences with the, 87; advantages of a free, 90
Bullion Report, the, 143

C

Canada, the Scotch system of banking in, 47
Capital, productiveness of, 50–52; but not money, belongs to the individual, 131; no superabundance of, possible, 134
Capital panic, a, how it works, 132
Changes in the currency of England, 103–105
Changes proposed, legislative, 32
Charles the First and Charles the Second of England break the eighth commandment, 13
China's, legal money, 38; use of silver, 38
Circulation, the, how to keep both the metals in, 19; what is meant by, 22
Clearing-house associations, development of, 66; an outcome of independent banking, 141

Clearing-house system, 53
Closing of the mints in India, 116
Coins of the Realm, Lord Liverpool's, 7, 107
Comptroller of the Currency of the United States for 1895, report of, 63
Conflict of the standards, 76
Contraction of credit, the cause of over-production, 127; causes of a, 128
Cost of production determines normal value, 89
Credit, distinctive function of, 159; misused, 159
Credit notes, what is meant by, 151
Crippled capital, 14
Currency, a self-regulative, 69; lack of, during a panic, 161
Currency panic, a, how it works, 132

D

Defects of the one-reserve system, 138, 140
Demand for silver money general, 5
Demonetization of silver, not over-production, the cause of decline in value, 86; in Germany, 95, 96; in India, 117, 119–121; stability of gold affected by, 121; a real grievance, 170
Dependence of one industry upon another, 128

Index

Disproportionate production different from over-production, 128

Dundee, Bank of, statement of, 59

E

Effect of the demonetization of silver in India, 117

Effect of a fixed ratio between silver and gold, 6

Effect of government discrimination as to its money, 69

Effect of making one metal represent another, 77

Elements which give stability to the precious metals, 81

England, Bank of, suspended specie payment, 106; the centre of the English banking system, 136, 137; founding of the, 136; first renewal of the charter of the, 137; Englishmen's faith in the, 138; notes are fiat money, 139; Issue and Banking departments of the, 150; notes are government money, 150; total issue of notes of the, 150; rate of discount of the, 166–168

England's, reasons for adopting the gold standard, 6; currency, changes in, 103–105; currency on a paper basis, 145; source of, commercial strength, 170

English economic literature, condition of, early in the nineteenth century, 144

English monetary system, the, 2, 136

Evolvement of a new system of metallic money, 108

Exchange of United States money at the Treasury, 68

F

Failure of our silver legislation, 78

Fixed capital, 54

Fixed ratio, effect of a, 6

Floating capital, 54; real owners of the nation's, 63; diversion of, 65, 157; function of, 159; during a panic, 161

France, action of the Bank of, 15, 97; wealth of, 98; hoarding of metallic money in, 98; branch banks in, 99

Free banking in Scotland, 45; in Canada, 47

Free coinage of silver, 2; effect of, on the silver-miner, 10; effect of, on the gold in the Treasury, 20; limit of, 25

G

Gold and silver monometallism contrasted, 109

Gold discoveries more probable than silver, 86

Gold, use of, in commerce, 102, 105; absorption of, 124

"Good" and "bad" money, 34

Government paper money, 3; popularity of, 70

Government savings-banks in Canada, 48, 49
Government's function, the, in supplying money, 24
Gravitation, law of, not accepted by the French nation, 36
Greenback, Party, the, 28; "craze," 29
Greenbacks and Treasury notes, what metal they represent, 74
Gresham Law, the, 34
Guinea, value of the, at different periods, 9

H

Hanson's, John S., tables of annual production of gold and silver, 83
How to keep both the metals in the circulation, 19, 21
Hybrid metallism, defined, 108; in Holland, 110–112; requirements of, 113; objections to, 126, 169

I

Immigration to the United States, 55
Importance of stability in money, 27; of a steady rate of interest, 135
India, closing of the mints in, 116
Individual banks contrasted with parent banks, 62, 64
International bimetallic league, 17
Issue department of the Bank of England, 150, 160

J

Jevons cited on the Gresham Law, 37, 39
Jones, Senator, views on silver, 11; on the advance in gold, 75

L

Latin Union, objects of the, 99; agreement of the, 100
Law regulating the issue of bank notes in England, 137
Legal tender, 13
Legislative changes proposed, 32, 68
Limit of bank-note issue, 57
Liverpool's, Lord, *Coins of the Realm*, 7, 107
Locke's, John, Essays on Money, 8; perception of the nature of money, 8; advice as to forcing gold into the circulation, 9

M

Malagrowther, Malachi, cited, 47
Misused credit, 159
Monetary reorganization, plan of, 1; indispensable features of a, 2
Monetary standard? What is a, 92
Monetary systems, of the world, 95; of the United States, 140
Monetary unit? What is a, 93
Monetary unit, of the United States, 93; of England, 93; of France, 93

Index

Money metals economized by the use of paper money, 129
Money not individual as capital is, 131
Money, true, 13; token, 14; the name, 21; productiveness of, 50; governed by the universal law, 70; distinctive function of, 159
Motive for the demonetization of silver, 124

N

National bank notes, 3; the redemption of, 42; elasticity of, 43
Negro's, the, preference for silver, 72
Newton, Sir Isaac, and the law of gravitation, 36; on the value of silver bullion and of the guinea, 104
New York banker, what a, says about panics, 132
New York, Stock Exchange of, 53; clearing-house system of, 53
Normal relative proportion of metallic and paper money, 71
Normal value determined by cost of production, 89
Number of State and National banks in the United States, 44

O

Objections to hybrid metallism, 126
One-reserve system, defects of, 138, 140; the result of exclusive privileges, 142
Opinions of mineralogists as to probable gold and silver discoveries, 86
Over-issue of bank notes, 152
Over-production the result of a contraction of credit, 127
Over-production of silver, not shown by statistics, 84; not the cause of its decline in value, 86
Over-trading and speculation, 153

P

Panics, of 1893, 29; cause of, 130; two kinds of, 130; panic of 1847, 156, 162; lack of currency during, 161; not unavoidable, 166
Paper money, government, 3; function of, 60; use of, economizes the money metals, 129
Parent banks contrasted with individual banks, 62, 64
Paris Monetary Convention, 92; business of the, 92; solution of the problem before the, 94
Parity of gold and silver dollars, how maintained, 20
Peel, Sir Robert, and the Scotch banks, 47; and the Bullion Report, 143; his object in securing the passage of the Banking Act, 149, 155; his theory of trade, 151
Plan of monetary reorganization, 1

Precious metals, the, as floating capital, 114; as reserve, 115
Problem, the, before the American people, 12
Production the final object of trade, 159
Productiveness of money, 50; of capital, 51
Proposed legislative changes, 32
Propositions, three, as to the redemption of United States money, 68

R

Railway building, 156; diversion of floating capital to, 158
Rate of discount of Bank of England, 166; changes in, 168
Redemption of United States money at the Treasury, 68
Relative stability of gold and silver, 88
Remonetization the remedy for demonetization, 123
Repeal of the Sherman Act, 31
Report of the United States Comptroller of Currency for 1895, 63
"Retired" national bank notes, 4
Rogers, J. E. T., cited, 114

S

Scotch system of banking, the, in Canada, 47
Scotland, free banking in, 45
Scott, Sir Walter, cited on Scotch banks, 46
Secretary of the Treasury, duties and powers of the, 68; as a banker, 73
Security more important than profit, 129
Self-regulating currency, a, 69
Sherman Act repealed, 31
Silver, free coinage of, 2; general demand for, 5; use of, 38; in the Treasury vaults, 78; currency of the, dollar, 93; coinage of, suspended in England, 106
Silver and gold monometallism contrasted, 109
Silver legislation, failure of our, 78
Silver question, the, how it may be settled, 171
Smith's, Adam, *Wealth of Nations*, 143
Soetbeer's, Prof., tables of production of the precious metals, 82, 84, 90, 101
Somers, Robert, cited on Scotch banking, 47
Speculation and over-trading, 153
Spencer, Herbert, cited on State control of the currency, 39
Stamp, true function of the, 7, 10
Standards, conflict of the, 76
Standard of value? What is a, 92
State money, 26
Stephenson, George, 156
Stock Exchange of New York, 35

Index

T

Ten-per-cent. Tax Bill, the, 28
Three propositions as to the redemption of United States money, 68
Token money, 14
Trading and over-trading, 152
Transport of the precious metals, 103
Transvaal, production of gold in the, 122
True function of the stamp, 7, 10
True money? What constitutes, 13

U

United States, monetary system of the, 140
Unit of account? What is a, 93
Unstable currency, evil effects of an, 155, 158

V

Value, of the guinea at different periods, 9; of the stamp, 79
Variation in the relative value of the precious metals, 80; causes of, 80

W

Wealth of Nations, Adam Smith's, 143

www.ingramcontent.com/pod-product-compliance
Lightning Source LLC
Chambersburg PA
CBHW020828190426
43197CB00037B/737